Bipolarized II

Bipolarized II

An Inside Guide to the "Other" Bipolar Disorder

Bink Books
Bedazzled Ink Publishing Company • Fairfield, California

978-1-949290-52-3 paperback

Cover photo
by
Ryan Johnson, Photographer
The Light Spell Studios
www.thelightspell.com

Cover design
by

The publisher gratefully acknowledges permission to cite material from the following sources:

Bipolar Disorder For Dummies, 3rd Edition (John Wiley & Sons, Inc., 2016), by Candida Fink, M.D., and Joe Kraynak,
M.A.
Chapter 6 quote ("Nobody understands . . ."), © 2019 PsychCentral.com. All rights reserved. Reprinted here with
permission.

Bink Books
a division of
Bedazzled Ink Publishing, LLC
Fairfield, California
http://www.bedazzledink.com

Dedication

To my fellow BP IIs. You know who you are.

Acknowledgments

I'm indebted to the following people, who helped in various ways and are thanked here alphabetically: Rachael Ackley, Tony Anderson, Mary Corder, Shaun Day, Sarah Ferrario, Diane Keith-Prohl, Brenda Lawson, Lorri S. Prohl, Kris Schwickrath, Andrew Simpson, and Jim VanNatta.

Reading life backward is a dicey proposition, but this book and I might not exist if not for the staff, volunteers, and fellow patients at Research Psychiatric Center, Kansas City, Missouri, and IU Health Methodist Hospital, Indianapolis, Indiana (then Methodist Hospital of Indiana). The same goes for the many excellent psychiatrists, counselors, and internists who've treated me over the years, including Dr. Amir Habib, Dr. Frederick Mittleman, Dr. Muhammed Munir, Vic Nelson, Carolyn Webster, and those whose names have vanished due to time and medication. Sincere thanks to you all.

Contents

Introduction:
Welcome to the Club

Rachael R. Ackley/H2O Design

ßΠ2

W e're not Dekes or Kappas or Chi Os, not SAEs, Phi Psis, or Tri Delts. We're not the Porc, Bones, or any of those.* Bipolar II is exclusive too, but no one wants to be tapped for it.

Bipolar disorder is mental illness. It's manic depression. It's serious.

If you've just been diagnosed, however, take heart: You haven't joined a secret society. We manic-depressives are everywhere (Chapter 4), and you already know some of us. *You're not alone.*

I could do worse than start by telling you about a famous emeritus member: Carrie Fisher. Yes, of course she was General Princess Leia, but I was always more a fan of the author. Her writing was witty, razor-sharp, and just the right kind of mordant. (I *like* mordant.) It spoke to me in unexpected, oddly familiar ways.

Only now do I understand why. Carrie Fisher had bipolar disorder, and now I know I do too.

* In order of mention: Delta Kappa Epsilon (ΔKE; fraternity), Kappa Kappa Gamma (KKΓ; sorority), Chi Omega (ΧΩ; sorority), Sigma Alpha Epsilon (ΣAE; fraternity), Phi Kappa Psi (ΦKΨ; fraternity), Delta Delta Delta (ΔΔΔ; sorority), Porcellian Club (Harvard University), and Skull and Bones (Yale University). If bipolar II were a Greek-letter organization, it would be Beta Pi 2 (βπβ′ or βπ2).

Fisher was open about her illness, lecturing and writing two nonfiction books about what she went through. She also wrote several novels, which she called *faction*, but they may have leaned toward fact. In 2004, at one of her lectures, I saw the unfinished tattoo above her downstage ankle—a supposedly fictional half-tattoo that her fictional heroine half-got in *The Best Awful*. True? False? Both?

Faction is a good description of a manic-depressive life.

There's a defining difference between her faction and mine, however: Fisher had bipolar I disorder, and I have bipolar II. My kind—*our* kind—is the focus of this book.

Why This?

Surprisingly little has been written about adult bipolar II (BP II) for the general public. The best-known trade books are about bipolar I (BP I). BP I (the one with mania) can manifest as extreme mood swings, crazed behavior, promiscuous use of sex and money, heavy drinking, recreational drugging, and/or staying awake for days. Not all cases fit this model, of course, but because bipolar I can be so dramatic, it gets more attention.

BP II (the one with hypomania) is every bit as severe but shorter on drama, which makes it harder to recognize, trickier to diagnose, and nowhere near as easy to write about. Few people seem to try outside medical journals.

This is too bad. If you look for books about our disorder, you find mostly arcane medical texts, celebrity-bipolar biographies, and earnest but dodgy self-published works. I wished that *someone* would write about BP II in a nonmedical, noncelebrity, antiearnest, undodgy, reasonably friendly way. That way, with luck, the content might be less alarming. With even more luck, it might be more useful to newly diagnosed BP IIs.

This book is my best shot at it.

How It Works

In keeping with the disorder, *Bipolarized II* is two books: a semimemoir and a manual of sorts. Most chapters mix brief personal stories with general info on the chapter topic: bite-size sidebars, tiny articles, and so on. Think of this book as an abridged version, not a definitive text.

Read whatever you want, in whatever order. If the sidebar title "Fish! Sunglasses! Mad Men!" upsets you (as it might), see how you feel about the chapter title "My Brain Hurts." If both upset you, maybe try not reading titles.

By the way:

- For the most part, bipolar disorder is aproached lightly herein, not because it's minor but because almost everything written about it is gloomy, doomy, and dry. Gloom isn't terribly helpful for manic-depressives, especially BP IIs.
- *Bipolar disorder* and *manic depression* are used interchangeably. The term *bipolars* turns up often too; it may not be a word, but it's easier to write (and read) than *people who have been diagnosed with bipolar disorder*.
- Although bipolarity comes in four generally recognized flavors (Chapter 4), this book deals primarily with BP II and to a lesser extent with BP I. Like adults, children can have any type, but pediatric bipolar disorder is beyond the scope of the book (except for sidebars in Chapter 2).
- Much as I approve of *they/them/their*, those pronouns were too hard to work into the book—certain memories are hard-wired—so gendered ones appear instead.
- Unavoidably, acronyms and footnotes crept into everything. Most acronyms are spelled out on first use and thereafter not; see Appendix A for definitions. As for the footnotes, most are little jokes on pedantry and easy to avoid.

- Finally, I'm no expert—only a Type 2 manic-depressive with a journalism background—so this book isn't medicoacademic, even though it draws on medical and academic research. **Neither is it meant to be *any* kind of medical advice, not even quackery.** It's simply some of what I found when I set out to research BP II. All I'm out to do is tell you a little about living with this illness, because not everyone who does wants to say.

One Last Thing

In the many years since my first diagnosis as unipolar depressive (wrong!), I went to Hell and back, Hell and back time and time again. Only after proper diagnosis and treatment did the round-trips to the underworld stop. I've come a long way and have farther to go, but life is better now.

It can be better for you too. Join the club.

bipolêre twee
Afrikaans

bipolarra bi
Basque

duie bipolari
Corsican

bipolære to
Danish

bipolaire twee
Dutch

du bipolaroj
Esperanto

bipolaarne kaks
Estonian

dalawang bipolar
Filipino

bipolaire deux
French

bipolare zwei
German

διπολικά δύο
dipoliká dýo
Greek

de bipolè
Haitian Creole

elua bipolar
Hawaiian

kétpólusú
Hungarian

tvíhverfa tveir
Icelandic

beirt bhipolar
Irish

bipolare due
Italian

bipolar duo
Latin

tuhinga o mua
Maori

bipolar dois
Portuguese

dhà dà-thaobhach
Scots Gaelic

bipolarna dva
Slovenian

laba laba-cirifood
Somali

dos bipolares
Spanish

bipolar mbili
Swahili

bipolära två
Swedish

iki kutuplu iki
Turkish

meji meji
Yoruba

i-bipolar ezimbili
Zulu

Hello my name is

Bipolar II

A II by Any Other Name

Not crazy about the term *bipolar II*? You're not wrong. It makes BP II sound like the Doublemint Doublemint Twins Twins of brainspeak; it lacks a certain *je ne sais quoi*. Why not try some of the following on instead?

Whoever undertakes to
set himself up as a judge
of Truth and Knowledge is
shipwrecked by the laughter
of the gods.
— Albert Einstein

Part 1

Not All There

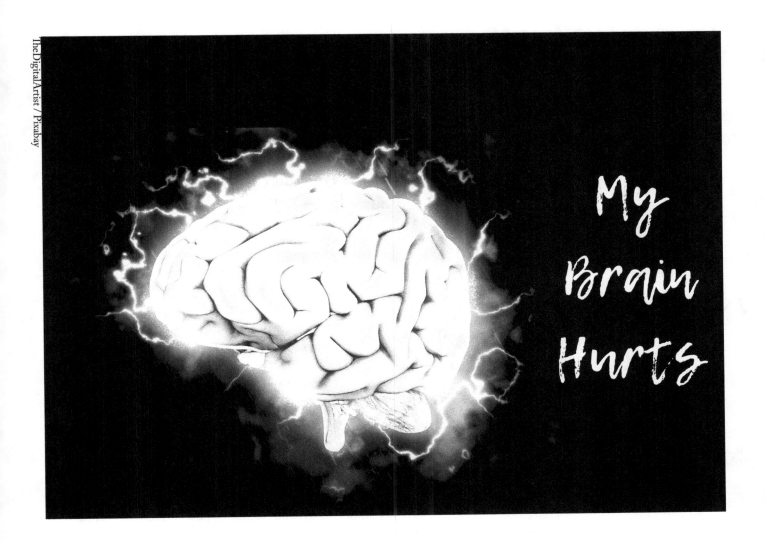

My Brain Hurts

As Roseanne Roseannadanna said on the original *Saturday Night Live*, it's always something. The something of this book is bipolar II disorder—BP II for short. Because it rarely travels alone, the book also covers a few comorbidities, the most common of which is attention-deficit/hyperactivity disorder, better known as ADHD.

(Roseannadanna again: It just goes to show you.)

Bipolar disorder is hard to explain to nonbipolars, most of whom can't even imagine it. Take sleep. The bipolar brain doesn't always want to. Many nights, mine can't turn off and keeps getting me up to take notes—most of which turn out to be illegible in the morning, partly because my handwriting is the despair of all who know me but mainly because of ADHD Brain, which is six years old when it's tired and can't write in cursive either. Something like this usually happens:

K.: Do you see what time it is?

BRAIN: Why?

K.: It's past our bedtime. We should be asleep.

BRAIN: Why?

K.: We're not doing this now. Good night. Go to sleep.

BRAIN: I don't want to.

K.: I don't care.

BRAIN: You're not the boss of me.

K.: I *am* you, dummy. Go to sleep.

BRAIN: Can't make me.

K.: Can.

BRAIN: Can't.

K.: Can.

BRAIN: Can't.

K.: C—

BRAIN: Can't, can't, infinity. Ha!

Rage, frustration, and getting out of bed again ensue.

BRAIN: What?

K.: I'm going to unscrew my head and take you out with a melon baller.

BRAIN: You don't have a melon baller.

K.: *I'll go buy one!!*

Brief silence.

BRAIN: Can we go to Starbucks while we're out?

Who Gets Bipolar Disorder?

Anyone could. Only 4 percent or so do. If anyone knew why, he or she would be the Archimedes of neuroscience.

Still, we do know a few things:

- Men and women are equally likely to develop bipolar disorder.
- The disorder occurs across races, ethnic groups, social classes, and ages around the world.
- The average age of onset is 25.
- More than two-thirds of manic-depressives have blood relatives who also have it or unipolar depression.

You can't tell by looking who's bipolar. It's a safe bet, though, that you know another bipolar, or know someone who does, or know someone who knows someone who does. Because Six Degrees of Kevin Bacon tells us that everyone is connected to everyone, including this fine actor.

To summarize, bipolar disorder is uncommon but universal, and if you don't know a fellow bipolar, you'll find one somewhere on the way to Mr. Bacon.

On a typical night, while all that goes on, Bipolar II Brain takes over the note-taking. It likes sleep best when it's depressed, which it isn't at the moment. It's irritable, which it often is when it isn't depressed. It wants to be busy more than it cares what the rest of us[**] are arguing about, so it gets busy as hard as it can.

Bipolar disorder and ADHD frequently co-exist but rarely in peace.

Suppose that you had this night. How do you think you'd feel in the morning? Now imagine that you had this night over and over—most of your adult life and about half your childhood (Part 1). How do you think you'd feel most days?

If you have bipolar disorder, you don't have to suppose or imagine. You've probably lived this scenario during manic or hypomanic cycles for as long as you can remember, even if you didn't have a name for what was going on with you.

I *had* the name, as it happened, but wouldn't use it. Why open such a big can of such crazy worms? Before diagnosis (Part 2), I explained my symptoms by saying, "My brain hurts."

In the Mood

You may already know this, but if not, here you go: Moods and emotions aren't the same.

A *mood* is a persistent or prolonged emotional state, such as irritability, whereas an *emotion* is a short-lived response, such as excitement. You might say that a mood is fixed, whereas an emotion is fleeting.

If you like this analogy better, an *emotion* is annoyance (how you feel when the alarm goes off and you realize that it's Monday), and a *mood* is despair (how you feel when you realize that there will be many more Mondays).

Or: An *emotion* is glee (acquiring a desirable luxury item), and a *mood* is contentment (having some limit left on your credit card).

Or: love vs. lust, and you come up with your own examples.

You'd have to ask a professional about the difference between those two things and feelings. To me, feelings are just the title of an atrocious 1975 song.[*]

[*] Nevertheless, Morris Albert's and Loulou Gasté's "Feelings" has been covered by many world-class singers, including Ella Fitzgerald, Sarah Vaughan, and Johnny Mathis. Also by Engelbert Humperdinck.

[**] Not *literally*. That would be schizophrenia.

In fact, it did hurt. *Does* hurt. Not literally, but pain all the same. Bipolar disorder is a roller coaster with no seat belts, so you keep banging your head: first up, then down, sideways on curves, upside down on loops. The more you ride—and there's no getting off—the more you bang your head. On hypomanic days, I can go from 0 to 60 to light speed and back in a minute or two (up, down, sideways, upside down).

On ADHD days, I can't watch a movie without getting up every few minutes to check my phone, to-do list, or Alexa (up, down, sideways, upside down). Depression is different but worse. This is not a painless way to live (Part 3).

The hard truth is that these roller-coaster switches are built-in settings, incurable and to some extent unchangeable. I'm on this ride for life.

The better truth is that the ride doesn't hurt so much nowadays. To string out this metaphor one time more than you want, I've got a lap

(Bipolar) II Is the Loneliest Number

According to the National Alliance on Mental Illness (NAMI), 20 percent of American adults experience some sort of mental illness each year. Very few of them are bipolar, though: Estimates range all over but generally fall between 2.4 and 4.4 percent of the population.

Unfortunately, these statistics don't seem to be broken down by category, so I couldn't find a hard-and-fast figure for BP II alone. But several studies estimate that its incidence is half that of BP I, so simple math would suggest that it affects about 1.2 to 2.2 percent of the population.

Adult ADHD (which often goes with bipolar disorder) is also rare among the general public, weighing in at 4 percent.

bar *and* a guardrail now. The bar might be meds and the rail could be information, or vice versa; it doesn't matter. The point is that I'm still going to get banged up, because that's life and because I'll still be manic-depressive, but now there's more protection.

My brain hurts less now.

And it only took years, miles, and oceans of trial and error to get here.

The process of learning to live with bipolar disorder is long because bipolar disorder is hard:

There's no such thing as a cure.

You can be better. With treatment, you can be stable. But you can never be an ex-bipolar.

You can't get to the bottom of it.

No one knows exactly what causes this illness, or who'll get it, or when, which goes especially hard on those of us who like solving puzzles. Some puzzles have no solutions, though, and bipolar disorder is one.

> The average human brain weighs 1,300 to 1,400 grams, or 2.866 to 3.086 pounds. By comparison, a goldfish brain clocks in at 0.097 gram, which translates to 2.138e-4 pounds. My brain is too small to comprehend the last number. (University of Washington)

You can't think or will yourself out of it.

If magical thinking worked, it would fix everything. Well, everything but manic depression. You can learn to control it to some extent, as one of my bipolar friends can (Chapter 13). But "curing" it with willpower or positivity isn't believable, achievable, or conceivable, no matter how hard you try.

If you *can* work this magic trick over the long term, I submit that you don't have bipolar disorder.

Fun as it is to say, our brains don't really hurt because they can't. More disturbing still, they're so incapable of feeling pain that neurosurgeons don't put patients to sleep during certain types of brain surgery. (Wu Tsai Neurosciences Institute, Stanford University)

The cycles are chronic and unpredictable.

Mania/hypomania and depression keep coming back, but not necessarily on a schedule. Some people have frequent mood swings, even rapid cycling (Chapter 8); others have only a few episodes over a lifetime. Some swings are triggered by external events; others have no apparent cause. But bipolarity cycles. Unless you're well stabilized, the unpredictability of this disorder can cause problems for you and everyone around you.

Medication can be trial-and-error.

No drug works for all bipolars and may not work at all for some. A change in dosage or schedule could make the difference. Arriving at efficacy may take a while, however; some meds require slow titration and/or don't take full effect for weeks.

Bipolar disorder affects almost everything.

Work, money, relationships, physical health, personal Zen—all (and more) are extra-challenging for bipolars because our disorder affects nearly every aspect of daily life.

Bipolar disorder can be lonely.

Even with the best will in the world, the people around you may struggle to understand your illness, let alone your behavior. The mood swings alone are confusing; it can be hard to tell an extremely good or bad mood from a manic/hypomanic or depressive episode. And let's face it: The stigma that's still attached to mental illness in general and manic depression in particular (Chapter 11) may frighten those who don't understand it.

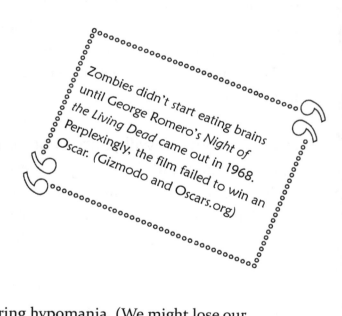

Zombies didn't start eating brains until George Romero's Night of the Living Dead came out in 1968. Perplexingly, the film failed to win an Oscar. (Gizmodo and Oscars.org)

BP II can be extra-bad.

We BP IIs don't have the disabling, sometimes-psychotic highs of BP I mania and don't lose control during hypomania. (We might lose our tempers or our car keys, of course.) Hypomania at least tends to be fun (Chapter 6). But we have deeper, longer-lasting depression, which is itself a serious illness and less than no fun.

Not exactly a week on the beach on the Riviera, is it? But bipolar disorder has been called the only mental illness with an up side—the ups—and you *can* live with it (Part 4). With a little help and a lot of commitment, so can your significant friends, relatives, and others. That's Part 5.

We can't blame all the misconceptions about our disorder on nonbipolars (whom I'll call *normals*, even though there's no such thing as normal). Too many of us have our own confused notions. Such as

- There's something wrong with me.
- So I must have done something wrong.
- It's a secret.
- So I should be ashamed.
- Uh-oh—maybe I'm crazy!

Tosh. Crazy is relative, as we know from our own relatives; the rest is perception. Look at this illness this way instead:

- Bipolar disorder is caused by brain chemistry, not character.
- You're born with the only brain you've got, which (like everything else you're born with) can malfunction.
- Your brain isn't user-serviceable.
- Even if it were, you couldn't get the parts.
- Any medical condition can be private, but secrecy and shame are optional.

There's no point denying it: Bipolar disorder is serious. Yet so are cancer, heart disease, and the other modern plagues, and you don't see people

xavi77 / Pixabay

The Fault Not in Our Stars

being ashamed of *them* or blaming themselves. If we could help being bipolar, we would. We can't, though. Accordingly, feeling guilty about our illness makes as much sense as feeling guilty about the Pleiades; we have nothing to do with them either. The fault is *not* in our stars.

I believe that our emotions are independent of our illness (see "In the Mood" in this chapter). We can be happy or sad like everyone else, for the same reasons and for reasons all our own. The problem isn't moods so much as mood regulation. Our wiring is such that our highs go higher and our lows go lower than most people's (sometimes to alarming extremes), and these highs and lows come and go like weather. Now and then, that weather is bad. But it's *still* not our fault.

This too: As the philosopher RuPaul says, "What other people think of me is none of my business."*

What other people think of you is none of your business.

If you find this truth helpful, stop reading. You get it. Go out for coffee or play Plants vs. Zombies or listen to *The Daily* instead.

If not, read on. With luck, you'll find something here that makes you feel at least a little better.

* RuPaul Charles, Twitter post March 1, 2011, accessed September 13, 2019. I'm not being snarky about the *philosopher* part.

Chapter 2

The Jabberwock in Elysium

John Tenniel illustration, *Through the Looking Glass* / public domain

. . . the gods intend you for [Elysium] . . . where all existence is a dream of ease. Snowfall is never known there, neither long frost of winter, nor torrential rain, but only mild and lulling airs from Ocean bearing refreshment for the souls of men—the West Wind always blowing.

—Homer, *The Odyssey*, 4:599-606

"The Jabberwock is the leading beast in "Jabberwocky," from Lewis Carroll's *Through the Looking Glass*. It burbled as it came whiffling through the tulgey wood but got snicker-snacked by a vorpal blade. You either like this stuff or you don't."

Some years ago, a younger friend complained that my people were too lucky. We didn't have to grow up with AIDS or crack, she said, and everything in life came too easy. Then—probably to make up for it—she said I was "cool for an old person."

I'll have you know that I was in my 30s at the time and still got carded. (Twice.) As for the rest, A. was half-right and half-wrong.

I grew up in the suburbs in the '60s, which may have been the best place and time to grow up ever; kids were everywhere, and everything was about us. I went to a brand-new elementary school, played in a brand-new park, lived in a brand-new house with an actual white picket fence. My peers and I were mostly unscheduled in our free time, with little adult supervision (the suburbs were almost too safe), so we had endless hours of unproductive fun. Which included the luxury—now extinct—of wasting time. We got to watch *lots* of cartoons.

We also taught ourselves useful things. To this day, I know how to tighten roller-skate toe clamps over a pair of canvas Keds, peel a cork liner cleanly out of a bottle cap, draw a hopscotch court on a sidewalk with a rock instead of chalk, clothespin a playing card to bicycle spokes to make it go pffffffffft when the wheel turns. These skills may be rare today, but every kid back then possessed them and kept them sharp.

Something else that came easy (by virtue of being born when we were) was optimism. We lived in exciting times, in a bright-shiny modern world. NASA was blasting off giant moon rockets at Cape Kennedy. Disneyland was open. Color TV was happening. We had transistor radios! We were Space Age children, already living in Tomorrowland, and the future was ours.

In short, I lived in Elysium.

Also not.

The price of this marvelous lifestyle, for my generation as for our parents', was conformity. You had to go along to get along, you *had* to get along, and God help the child who didn't. If even God wouldn't help you, you needed luck.

I may have grown up in a fortunate way, in a fortunate time, but luck—and my brain—weren't with me. The brain made me Different.

The good news: I could read by age three and was skipped to second grade halfway through first. That was also the bad news.

More bad: I never had to study, so no one ever found out I couldn't.

It won't surprise you to learn that I was a weird kid. One year in grade school, we had to memorize and recite a poem of our choice. Most of the class picked limericks, but I chose Lewis Carroll's "The Walrus and the Carpenter," which I guess was showing off. So of course I was bullied from second grade through senior year. The Plastics in *Mean Girls* were nothing next to those jerks.

Being bullied for weird was hard; not knowing *why* I was weird was harder. We're not talking personality alone. Some days, I talked a blue streak; others, I sulked nonstop. There was never much telling which way things would go. Once, I threw an operatic tantrum because Mom and Dad wouldn't let me watch *Batman* and had to be carried out of the living room literally kicking and screaming. The teenage version was stomping upstairs and slamming my bedroom door so hard that the windows rattled.

School wasn't much better. Most classes were so boring that I couldn't focus on whatever the teachers were saying (and usually knew the material already, having read everything within reach), so I wrote poems and plays in class instead. Not good ones. In eighth grade, I also drew and wrote a comic strip. Also not good. It was snarky, mean, and awful, the way I was starting to feel.

Then it got worse: puberty.

Now, puberty is no fun for anyone; I've always said that junior high is punishment in advance for whatever we're going to do next. In my case, though, the changes were unwanted, and they brought company.

My teens *hurt*. I was horribly uncomfortable in my skin. Listening was a problem; not interrupting was a problem; controlling my increasingly hot temper was a problem. Also, I was starting to have trouble with noise. Yes, our house was loud, what with two teenagers and a preteen blasting three stereos upstairs, a younger sibling learning to play the piano downstairs, and four sets of friends in and out day and night. *My* noise was always fine, you understand, but anyone else's was a federal offense.

By senior year, I was mad at everyone at home, almost everyone at school, and myself for growing up. This wasn't what I'd signed on for. It wasn't fair.

How had things gone so wrong? What happened to Elysium?

Even though more doctors are wise to pediatric bipolar disorder these days, diagnosis can still take years. Generally, though, the following symptoms tend to characterize bipolar children:

Portrait
of the
Bipolar
As a
Young Child

Severe, unusual mood swings
Hyperactive/impulsive or reckless behavior
Aggression
Trouble sleeping
Unusual sadness or irritability
Very fast, rambling speech

Poor control of temper
Grandiose behavior
Hypersexuality or other inappropriate behavior
Lack of focus
High distractibility

Although this list isn't broken down by bipolar I and bipolar II, the same pattern tends to apply: more extreme mood swings in BP I, longer depression and shorter well periods in BP II.

As in adults, diagnosis can be difficult because many other childhood disorders resemble bipolar, especially ADHD, major depression, anxiety, and ODD (Chapter 5).

We're all experts on the past, or think we are, but here's some of what may have been up with my young self:*

- Unipolar depression (bipolar disorder usually sets in later; see Chapter 7)
- ADHD
- Anxiety
- Delayed emotional development
- Social immaturity and general cluelessness
- The onset of high sensitivity
- A touch of oppositional defiant disorder (ODD)

High sensitivity is real enough, but some people doubt that ODD is a thing. I'm not sold on it either; some kids are natural brats. Still, I was at war with Mom and Dad from junior high on. Not so much with teachers—not openly, not then. Only recently did I unrepress my anger at Mr. H., who chose someone else for yearbook editor-in-chief my senior year. (Do you know who he picked instead? A dweeb with zero experience who didn't even *go* into journalism later.) I'm still mad about missing journalism camp at Indiana University that summer; it was only for editors-in-chief.

The same month I started consciously hating Mr. H. again, I essentially told my whole high-school class to go to hell—not once, but *twice*.

Like Liz Lemon on *30 Rock*, however, I may misremember a little. Lately, I've also begun to recall saying very mean things about anyone—teacher, student, or random stranger—who dared to cross me during those years. I remember now, too, drawing cartoons of a loathsome junior-high gym teacher, poking pencil holes in her face to simulate zits, and then (to aid the slow-witted) labeling them ZITS. I accidentally dropped the comic-strip notebook in the gym one day. Karma is real: The gym teacher found the notebook, and read it, and punished me for it for the rest of the school year.

> British and Swedish researchers have discovered a link between bipolarity and high IQ: Young people who were straight-A students had a fourfold higher risk than their peers of developing bipolar disorder. Those who excelled in music, humanities, science, and (for some reason) Swedish ran the greatest risk. As often happens, all the subjects were boys, which is regrettable; smart girls get bipolar disorder too. (*The British Journal of Psychiatry*)

It's just barely possible that I was a bit of a shit and that these people were human. It's certain that I had no brakes and was up or Gothically down most of the time. This sounds a little bipolar.

(I'm not wrong about *everyone* from back then, though.)

—Where were we? Right: probable childhood problems. Not all of them were/are medical, but what difference would it have made? Almost no one knew about bipolar disorder at the time, much less ADHD, and even if my parents or other adults *had* known, they couldn't have helped. As far as anyone knew, including me, the trouble was being persistently weird. Nobody got me. Nobody wanted to.

I was the Jabberwock. Lots of young bipolars-to-be are.

Risky Bipolar Business

A few more reasons why bipolar children need accurate diagnosis, stat:

- Half of all chronic mental illness begins by age 14, and three-quarters starts by 24.
- Each year that bipolar children are undiagnosed and untreated, their odds of recovery go down by 10 percent.
- Bipolar disorder may be at least partly genetic. One journal of psychiatry estimates the risk of inheritance as follows:
  - *One parent with bipolar disorder*: 15 to 30 percent risk for each child
  - *Both parents with bipolar disorder*: 50 to 75 percent risk for each child
  - *Siblings and fraternal twins*: 15 to 25 percent risk
  - *Identical twins*: ±70 percent risk

The one benefit of being weird, bullied, and Jabberwocky is that it toughens you up. In first/second grade, I was a small, defenseless 6-year-old; by senior year, I was Xena, but meana. Still, I wasn't "normal."

That was fine. I was starting to hate my "normal" classmates back anyway.

Maybe college would be better.

* This list isn't self-diagnosis (for reasons explained in Chapter 4)—only conjecture.

It's Not Me, Kid; It's You

MabelAmber / Pixabay

"Your face is going to freeze that way."

I know one thing about you for a fact: You got lots of criticism while you were growing up. The reason I know this is that bipolar disorder rarely manifests itself until a person's teens or 20s (average age: 25), so the vast majority of bipolars went undiagnosed as children. Most of us already exhibited symptoms, though. Which means that unless your parents were Ward and June Cleaver—or Phil and Claire Dunphy on a good day—they probably came down hard on you for what you couldn't explain, much less control.

Mine did. Did they ever! My symptoms started with adolescence, which tends to be hard on all teens and parents but was brutal for me and mine. Years later, the Myers-Briggs test (Chapter 10) explained more than therapy did. Turned out that I'm an INFP and Mom was a simon-pure ESTJ—exactly the opposite. By the time I was 13, we understood each other about as well as an arts major and a Masai warrior and clashed nearly as often. (Dad didn't get involved, having known Mom longer and better.)

So I got an earful and then some of certain editorial comments. Didn't you?

- "It's your fault / imagination / bad temper / bad personality."
- "You're too sensitive / selfish / private / antisocial."
- "I don't know what goes on in that head of yours."
- "I don't care what you feel like."
- "You have a bad attitude."
- "Quit being so dramatic."
- "Wipe that look off your face."
- "Your face is going to freeze that way."
- "You catch more flies with honey than vinegar." (**Note:** I didn't want flies.)
- "Pay attention when I'm talking to you."
- "Don't talk back to me."
- "Go to your room until you adjust that attitude."
- "Come out of your room and talk to the rest of us."
- "Stop fidgeting."
- "Snap out of it."

Now that you know you're BP II, you can match most of these comments with symptoms: talking back, acting out, and fidgeting for hypomania; sensitivity, isolation, and vinegar for depression. Now that you're older, you may even suspect that your parents said those things out of confusion and worry. So did mine.

That doesn't mean we have to like it. As bipolar IIs, we're prone to greater rejection sensitivity than other bipolars, mostly when we're depressed. It hurts to be rejected by anyone; it takes time to recover. But rejection by one's parents during childhood—even if temporarily, even if driven by fear—may be irremediable. This kind of rejection can leave wounds that never quite heal.

It's OK to resent the preceding comments. It's understandable to react badly if you get them as an adult. To some extent, we're the same way now that we were then, especially during peak highs and lows, so we still can't help everything we say, do, and think. Being human, we may lash back when attacked, especially over hard-wired traits we were born with and can't change.

If you get putdowns like these on a regular basis, you might need better friends. Or you may want to try therapy. Otherwise, I have no advice. Criticism may be meant to be constructive but rarely is, and if you know a way to take it gracefully, let me know.

Chapter 3
Bipolar Vortex

So: maybe college would be better. Then, after college, adult life would be better. Everyone said so; I had no reason to doubt them. But I've learned one thing since: When in doubt, *doubt*.

In what follows, you may see patterns that suggest bipolarity. You may also see why I couldn't. I've learned this too: You can't see what your brain is up to from inside your head.

Michael Drummond / Pixabay

My first day at Indiana University, I'd been seventeen for only a few days and had no idea what to expect. I wish I'd expected my roommate, who couldn't have been a worse fit; or the walking distances on campus; or the classes, which were horrifying surprises. (So much homework!) I'd taken advanced-placement tests that spring and tested out of college English; unfortunately, I'd tested out of first-year French too. Two minutes into French 201, I realized that the professor might as well have been speaking Greek. (In French.) I was in multiple trouble from Day 1.

This happens to college freshmen; this is what it's *like*. Most people survive the transition. But most people don't have undiagnosed mental disorders. The shock of starting college was brutal for someone too young and naïve to be there, let alone ill and getting worse. By the second week, I was severely depressed and quit going to classes.

Guess what happened.

Mom and Dad were *furious*.

The next fall, I tried again at Ball State University, where two of my best friends from high school went. The first thing I did—the first thing *everyone* did—was buy a BALL U T-shirt. Besides the funny shirt, I had a private room in the dorm, where this time, people were friendly. Well, of *course* they were; it was the party dorm. Would it help to tell you that our floor had the lowest cumulative GPA on campus that year?

Soon, I'd switched out the high-school friends for the new friends and for beer, pot, and more pot. I went to lots of parties, sang and played guitar at all hours, and decided to be a rock star when (if) I grew up. For the first time, college was *fun*. Life was good.

"What about classes?" you ask. What about them? I took easy ones and went often enough to scrape passing grades at first—scraped because I *still* never studied. Then spring quarter came, and I never set foot in class again.

Guess what happened twice.

Mom and Dad were furiouser the second time and made me pay back every cent of my college loans. It took a few years to work off the debt— a fact that would shock a therapist one day. "Parents don't make their children pay them back for college," she insisted. (Don't they? Really? Did my parents know that?)

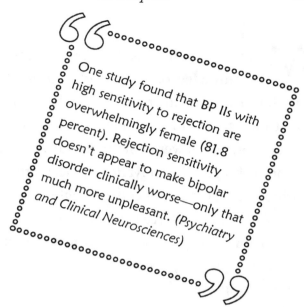

One study found that BP IIs with high sensitivity to rejection are overwhelmingly female (81.8 percent). Rejection sensitivity doesn't appear to make bipolar disorder clinically worse—only that much more unpleasant. (*Psychiatry and Clinical Neurosciences*)

Later, I tried one last time at IU, paying my own way. But I ran out of money much faster than expected, which was depressing, and what with being depressed, I cut classes.

Guess what happened three times.

The problem with me and college was part immaturity; part lack of preparation; and part wrong places, wrong times. But the largest part may have been undiagnosed mental illness. My brain was always confused and overwhelmed in those early postadolescent years, and when your brain's in that state, you don't know that something's wrong, or what, or how much. Besides, how can you fix what you don't know is broken?

My broken brain said we'd had enough college and who needed a degree anyway, and of course I believed it. (Would my own brain lie to me?) College had at least given me social skills and a light patina of extroversion; now those skills would help me get jobs I had no business getting. Then I could fake the rest.

Maybe adult life *would* be better.

The Yuppie-Scum Years

Synchronicity, dumb luck, or (at long last) right places, right times were on my side for a while. I'd gone to college to be a journalist, and there I was one after all, even without a degree. Publishing paid a living wage then; better, it was fun. So were most of my co-workers. Before long, I took on the protective coloring of our profession and became Yuppie Scum.

It was almost perfect. My first publishing job was the most stressful, but it was the best. Editorial and production pulled all-nighters, extracted giant rabbits from tiny hats on deadline, and read bluelines at 2 a.m. in a small room where an art director was throwing X-Acto knives at the wall. I *loved* this. I swear to you that all of it—even the flying knives—was fun. You can see yourself that I should have stayed put.

But ambition got the better of me (see: Yuppie Scum), which is why I wound up at a division of Paramount a few years later. Yes, that Paramount. The division was tech-book publishing, and I tell you truly, it put the *dead* in *deadline*. No one read proofs in the small hours; no one threw knives in the art department. I don't think anyone even punched a partition after a fight with the publisher and broke the partition *and* his hand. (That happened.) Work had become galactically less fun.

For a while, I coped by drinking too much coffee and blasting New Wave on my Walkman. Later, to make a point, I tacked a *Bram Stoker's Dracula* poster over my desk

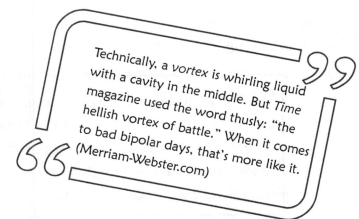

Technically, a vortex is whirling liquid with a cavity in the middle. But *Time* magazine used the word thusly: "the hellish vortex of battle." When it comes to bad bipolar days, that's more like it. (Merriam-Webster.com)

and drew fangs on the smiley face that a co-worker had taped to my office door. He did it as a joke, but I'd asked for it, having been a bat for weeks. The rest of the staff gave me the benefit of the doubt because they swore my office was cursed. Not out of the question: The last editor who'd occupied it had a nervous breakdown and never came back to work. I liked the idea of having a cursed office, to tell you the truth.

Then I had my own nervous breakdown and wound up in the hospital.

By the way, that was the second time. (See "Down the Hatch" in this chapter.)

I'd done years of therapy by then and thought whatever was wrong had been cured. Who knew the problem was bipolar disorder? Who knew it *couldn't* be cured? Some hospital doctors confidently diagnosed major depression and prescribed antidepressants that made things worse, which should have told those mallards something (Chapter 4). But all they did was refer me to mallards on the outside who diagnosed major depression again and prescribed more antidepressants, including one that kicked me into mania and one that almost killed me (Chapter 9). Many more pills of all shapes, sizes, colors, and indications followed; none worked. I was getting even worse.

Do you wonder why?

After That

It would make a better story to say that I hit bottom at that point, with nowhere to go but up. More went wrong, though. Lots more.

> The Ball family, of canning-jar fame, donated what would become Ball State University to the state of Indiana. Later, they also donated artworks to the campus art museum. It may not be true, as everyone swears, that one painting donated by the family had a plaque that read *Hung by the Balls*. But I hope so.

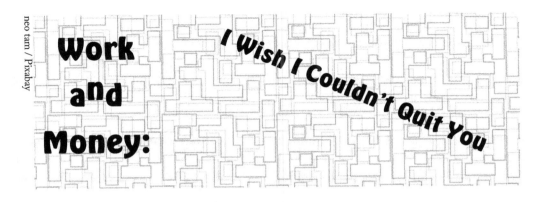

Work and Money: I Wish I Couldn't Quit You

Work

You may find this inconceivable, but during my first magazine job, I sulked through a long Fourth of July weekend because it meant not working for three days. Who *was* that person?

Not the same one who cracked up in the corporate publishing job, that's for sure. The hospital had done some good (see "Down the Hatch" in this chapter), but the aftermath undid it. One day, I lost a few marbles and told off a supervisor I didn't like. That didn't help, but it didn't get me fired either.

Finally, I quit the job.

Again.

Did I mention that I'd quit a *lot* of jobs? By my best calculation, I've had 34 and quit 29. The rest I was fired from, mostly for cause.

I'd always had trouble with authority figures but tried to put up with the bosses' crazy ideas because they paid me. But even this tiniest bit of tolerance wasn't sustainable. Bosses also had some notion that they could micromanage me every last fucking minute, which had a way of enraging me. I was bad at accessing most emotions but *great* at rage, which came out of nowhere—an impulse I couldn't resist and didn't try to. I got mad, and then I quit.

Does this sound familiar?

This coping mechanism finally broke down because hiring managers can read. As my résumé grew longer, explaining it became more complicated and new jobs got harder to get. Before long, I was unemployed, unemployable, and broke.

If this sounds like picturesque fun, I'm not telling it right.

Bipolar effect: Almost certainly hypomania, manifested by impulsivity, irritability, impaired judgment, and reckless financial choices; also depression from the fallout from hypomanic episodes.

The research: Bipolar job misery seems to love company. One study found that 54 percent of bipolar respondents had been fired or laid off; two others reported a 60 percent unemployment rate. Absenteeism is often a contributing factor, in that bipolars are seven times more likely than others to miss work due to illness.

Money

To recap: I had none, even with a steady income. Math was never my thing, and who cared anyway?

I came by this attitude semihonestly because Mom and Dad often stressed out loud about money at dinnertime. My takeaway: money = bad.

Not long ago, one of my brothers and I talked about those dinner-table conversations. He said they motivated him; he grew up determined to make good money and to handle it carefully. (He met those goals.) But those same conversations depressed me. If you worked hard but couldn't always make ends meet, why bother? I decided not to. (*I* met *that* goal.)

Consequently, I thought money was for spending. I could blow through a credit limit without a second thought, or a first one, because when I want something, I *want* it. To a hypomaniac, *now* means the day before yesterday. *Now* is too late.

Doesn't this sound bipolar too?

Bipolar effect: Definite hypomania, verging on just plain mania, with impulsivity, grandiosity, recklessness, and (very) poor judgment.

The research: When it comes to the effect of unemployment on a person's finances, you can do the math yourself. Here are a few expert findings, though: As many as 40 percent of bipolars need inpatient care at least once; after discharge, most of them see a psychiatrist every month or so for medication management; and almost everyone who has bipolar disorder needs medication. The costs of all these treatments vary but usually vary high.

Bad Romance

Is it OK with you if we don't talk about this part much? We all have some damage. This damage is as old as the sheer hell of high school, which almost everyone, bipolar and not, can relate to.

I'm no exception. From high school on, so many people messed with my head—which was messed up enough already—that I had to shut it down. A life without a bad romance or two or twenty is still a life. But now and then, I wish I'd made a few of those missed connections; they might have made lovely memories.

Bipolar effect: Long-term depression, indecisiveness, anhedonia, inappropriate guilt, occasional suicidal thoughts.

The research: Relationship problems are status quo for bipolars. In one study, 65 percent said they had trouble maintaining long-term relationships, and 34 percent were separated or divorced. Another study found that nearly 38 percent of depressed BP IIs experienced rejection sensitivity to such an extent that it destabilized their relationships and caused them to avoid future ones for fear of further rejection.

If there are studies of how having your head messed with affects happily-ever-after for manic-depressives, I haven't found them.

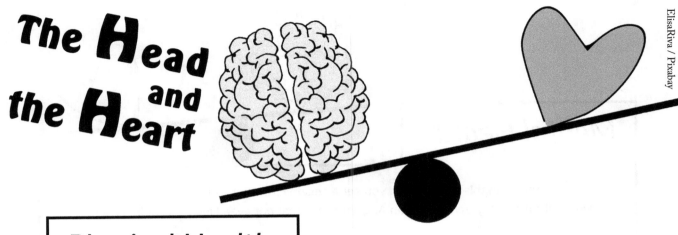

The Head and the Heart

Physical Health

I've already said that growing up was physically, literally painful (Chapter 2), and the being-uncomfortable-in-my-skin part got worse over time. Being me was like wearing a straitjacket that didn't even fit right. Like Anne Rice's vampires in *The Tale of the Body Thief*, I'd have switched bodies in a trice—and given that option today, I still might.

Regrettably, I wasn't a vampire. (Still not one.) Furthermore, I was healthy inside the uncomfortable skin. Most likely, some somatic acting-out was going on, with the mind taking its frustrations out on the body. Nothing was lastingly damaging, but nothing was fun.

Bipolar effect: Hypomania (irritable), depression, and hypochondria.

The research: In addition to having a high rate of comorbid mental illnesses (Chapter 5), manic-depressives are at extra risk of cardiovascular disease, obesity (from sedentary lifestyles and/or psychiatric drugs), and self-medication. That last one can include anything from a hard-core cheeseburger habit to marathon gaming to ruinous shopping. Whatever gets you through the night. The most popular substances for abuse purposes, however, are alcohol (more in BP I than in BP II), drugs illegal and otherwise, and cigarettes.

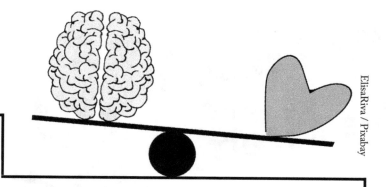

Mental Health

Add up everything in this chapter, and you get a negative result. Work, money, love/sex, physical well-being—all a mess. My psyche was an Augean stable that not even Hercules could have mucked out.

After three hospitalizations and years of talk therapy, after buckets of pills and thousands of bucks, how could I *not* be any better?

It's still a good question. For too many years, doctors and therapists failed to see what was right in front of them: a manic-depressive with unmistakable symptoms. They all had access to the *DSM* (Chapter 4); presumably, they'd heard the term *manic depression*. Maybe they thought it wasn't bipolar disorder or that bipolar was something else.

Or maybe the disorder outwitted them.

In *A Brilliant Madness*, Oscar-winning actor Patty Duke described fooling doctor after doctor with charm and what she called the cleverness of manic depression. It *can* be diabolically clever. The disorder helped me figure out therapy fast, and together, we figured out how to game it. We also had the help of ADHD, which enables some of us to see around the corners of conversations (Chapter 5). I'm not proud to say that I still know how to misdirect therapists because my illnesses still know how.

But I wish my bipolar disorder had been dumber, because we wasted years playing games. I wanted help but wanted to fool the doctors more.

Bipolar effect: Hypomania with grandiosity, euphoria, and irritability; depression with despair.

The research: You can find statistics on the mental effects of bipolar disorder throughout this book, but especially in Part 3.

Down n the Hatch

Many people are frightened of psychiatric hospitals. Perfectly understandable. What goes on inside is private, a/k/a secret, which means unknown. Mental illness can be the Devil, but the one you *don't* know is the bad one.

I met that one the day a doctor said he'd have to admit me to a mental hospital. I was almost too sick by then to be scared, but only almost.

Funny thing, though—the hospital (booby hatch? loony bin? funny farm? nuthouse?) wasn't so scary after all. Also, it saved my life.

I can't tell you everything about that first hospitalization, mostly to protect the privacy of the other patients. What I *can* tell you is this.

> **Note:** Not all psychiatric hospitals are equal; not every patient has a positive experience. I was lucky enough to have good insurance, which got me into first-rate facilities.

The hospital was like an ordinary hospital.

You couldn't tell much difference except that a few doors were locked and the patients wore street clothes. You might even have mistaken it for a plush rehab. That hospital had a gym, a large sunroom, a TV lounge, and a pleasant shaded patio—the perfect place to hang with all those new friends. (It was summer.)

The hospital was like school.

We didn't have classes exactly, but we were booked up all day every day: meds, breakfast, individual therapy, group therapy, lunch, arts and crafts, more group therapy, dinner, recreation, and meds. Or something like that. We also had frequent check-ins with nurses.

I understand now that keeping us busy kept us out of trouble—and under the eye of the staff—but the tight structure and group activities were also therapeutic. Most of us were depressed, and when you're really depressed, you shouldn't be alone with your brain.

I was really depressed.

Some of it was fun.

Strange as it may sound, my stay in that first psychiatric hospital not only saved my life, but also changed it for the better. While there, I learned that no one makes better friends than people, that sleeping all night is restful, and that I shouldn't believe everything I think. (Still learning that last one.)

More than that, much of that time was more fun than you'd think possible. Most of us were young and had a lot in common besides being mentally ill, so we bonded. One afternoon, a few nurses took those of us who had passes to see *Legal Eagles* downtown; it was a forgettable movie (I don't remember a frame of it now) but a crazy-fun road trip. Later that week, we got up a game of volleyball, which quickly morphed into psychodrama. It was a road-company production of *Les Misérables*, really, but with less misère and more Prozac, and we laughed about it even at the time.

Just now, I've also remembered a night after evening meds. A hospital friend and I went out to the patio to smoke and wait for the sleeping pills to kick in. They kicked in *way* sooner than we expected. We didn't want to go in, though, so we stayed out there as long as we could, laughing, talking, getting sleepier and dumber and then downright stupid, and laughing even harder. I've never felt closer to anyone I've just met.

Maybe you had to be there. But I have some awfully good memories.

None of it was perfect.

There were down sides, of course. One was that the patients weren't allowed to take photos or exchange phone numbers. When I asked one of the therapists why, she explained that it was a matter of privacy. I get that, absolutely. But I also hate having had to lose touch with those people. We went through a deep, profound experience together, and I wonder to this day how their lives have worked out.

More serious was the fact that the hospital missed my diagnosis (Chapter 4). I understand that too, sort of. My presenting symptom was severe, suicidal depression, and as far as anyone knew, I'd never had a manic episode. The problem was that during my stay, I cycled. Early in the second week, an overpowering wave of energy and almost supernatural well-being washed over me out of nowhere, combined with a deep-dish calm I'd never experienced before. Suddenly, I felt healthy, centered, enlightened, *better*. So much better, in fact, that the hospital discharged me a few days later—two weeks ahead of plan.

That energy blast must have been my first true hypomanic episode. I'm not complaining; it got me discharged early, and it was fantastic while it lasted. But how could all those doctors admit a severely depressed person one week and release a euphoric version of that same person the very next week *without* suspecting manic depression? The right diagnosis then might have saved years of pain and two more hospitalizations.

All of it was worth it.

Despite the less-than-great parts, I'll always be grateful for the experience. For one thing, mental hospitals hold no terrors anymore. I've been there, done that three times now, and those hospitalizations helped me get better.

True, I saw things that will haunt me for life and that I won't tell you—or anyone, *ever*. People are admitted to psychiatric hospitals for a reason.

I was off my own rocker too, in a way. The admitting nurses took away my razor and nail clippers so I couldn't use them to hurt myself; they kept me locked on the ward for the first three days; I had extra check-ins at first. Suicidally depressed people are *also* admitted to psychiatric hospitals for a reason.

But the fact that I'm here to write this book is proof that hospitalization was worth it—all of it. In the end, it wasn't so bad to crack up. Cracks let air and sunlight in.

Part 2

Finding Out

Chapter 4

All in Your Head: Diagnosis

"Well, *there's* your problem."

Childhood and early adulthood were a mess, then (Part 1), what with the hospitalizations, deadly meds, and suicidal thinking, not to mention the troubles in every single major area of life. Could it *get* any worse?

Sure it could. And did. Except for changes in music, fashion, and presidents, the years were starting to seem interchangeable, and interchangeably bad. I still didn't know what I hadn't known ten years before, and if I'd learned anything from any mistake, it went up in flames with the next one. Polish activist (later president) Lech Walesa once told *Time* magazine about looking back on "ruins and things burned out," which pretty well described the view in my own rearview mirror. I doubted that the road ahead would look any different.

You can trust me.

I'm a doctor.

It didn't. Crisis succeeded crisis with perfect regularity; spinout followed spinout; you could almost set your watch. My health began to crack under the stress, as health does. Soon, I was in and out of doctors' offices, asking for—*demanding*—a miracle in a pill.

That miracle came in the end, but not in a pill. During an appointment for yet another psychosomatic complaint, Dr. H. said, "You know, you might have the same situation as one of my other patients." That patient had a mood disorder, he said, along with ADHD, and treatment had changed her life. He thought maybe his friend Dr. M. could help me too.

Diagnosis can be tricky for manic-depressives. Most of us—*69 percent*, according to one study—are misdiagnosed, and these misdiagnoses can go on for a shockingly long time. More than a third of us wait 10 years or more to get proper diagnosis and treatment; the average wait is *17 years*. Also on average, bipolars get more than three incorrect diagnoses and see at least four doctors first.

I'm emphasizing these statistics because I lived them. For decades, doctors misdiagnosed me with unipolar major depression (despite the hypomanic episodes), along with panic attacks (which I never had). Until Dr. H., no one even suspected comorbid ADHD.

Still, those doctors weren't necessarily wrong. Undiagnosed bipolars tend to seek help when they're depressed, not when they're manic or hypomanic. (Mania and hypomania feel *great*.) For this reason, doctors tend to see only the depressive part of the cycle. Further, many patients underreport symptoms because they're scared of the stigma of a mental-health diagnosis. Finally, in bipolar II, the downs are much longer and more severe than the ups, capable of lasting as long as five years, especially during the early stages of illness. All those features can lead physicians to draw the wrong conclusion based on presentation.

> More than 80 percent of cases of bipolar disorder are classified as severe, and untreated bipolar disorder usually gets worse. (NAMI)

All that was true for me.

Yet another impediment to diagnosis is comorbidity (Chapter 5). In fact, co-occurring psychiatric illnesses are the norm in manic depression. More than half of undiagnosed bipolars have anxiety disorders of some sort, and mania/hypomania can masquerade as anxiety. ADHD interferes with concentration; so do mania/hypomania and depression. The puzzle box has even more interlocking levels, because bipolar cycles themselves may have overlapping symptoms. What's more, mood cycles aren't monolithic; there can be short periods of relief during depression and short periods of calm during hypomania, the key word being *short*.

All that was true for me too.

> Without treatment, manic/hypomanic cycles can last 3 to 6 months; depressive cycles, 6 to 12 months. (NHS England)

There's no blood test for manic depression. It doesn't show up on a microscope slide or in an X-ray, not even in an MRI or CAT scan. Instead, doctors usually go by a combination of patient history, reported symptoms, and observed symptoms. The history alone may hold important clues; problems with relationships and work, financial and/or legal issues, and substance abuse are common (but not universal) in bipolar disorder.

Some doctors also employ questionnaires. Anyone can find "Are You Bipolar?" quizzes on the Internet, to be sure, but med school is supposed to teach physicians to know better. (*You* should know better too; see "A Fool for a Doctor: Self-Diagnosis" in this chapter.) Instead, doctors can turn to an inexhaustible variety of diagnostic tools, such as the Tri-Axial Bipolar Spectrum Screening Quiz, the Bipolar Spectrum

Diagnostic Scale, the Schedule for Affective Disorders and Schizophrenia, the Mood Disorder Questionnaire, or (if we've suddenly gone back to the '90s) the Goldberg Bipolar Spectrum Screening Quiz. Arguably, however, the best current yardsticks are *The Diagnostic and Statistical Manual of Mental Disorders*, 5th Edition (*DSM-5*), and the Structured Clinical Interview for *DSM-5* (SCID-5 for short).

I think that Dr. M. used a combination of history, interview, and expert know-how with me. Identifying a mood disorder took him about 15 minutes.

"I don't want you to concentrate too much on the diagnosis," he said when I asked what kind. But I *wanted* to concentrate too much, so it was the work of a moment to look up the med he prescribed and arrive at bipolar II.

Later, I did more research and found that my history checked every single box on the BP II checklist.

Also, I made Dr. M. confirm it last summer.

The road to ADHD diagnosis took a different route. Two members of my family were diagnosed with it at about the same time, and because ADHD often runs in families, like manic depression (Chapter 2), it seemed like a good idea to get checked. So I made an appointment with a psychologist.

The ADHD screening took all morning. First was a computer game of sorts that resembled Pong; every time a small line appeared onscreen, I clicked a clicker. There followed a variety of memory, drawing, and other tests, including two mentioned in Chapter 10: the second edition of the Minnesota Multiphasic Personality Inventory (MMPI-2) and the third edition of the Milon Clinical Multiaxial Inventory (MCMI-III). A lengthy personal interview wrapped everything up.

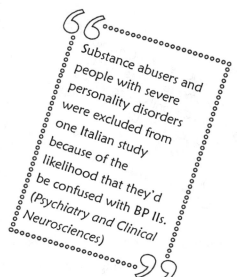

"Substance abusers and people with severe personality disorders were excluded from one Italian study because of the likelihood that they'd be confused with BP IIs. (*Psychiatry and Clinical Neurosciences*)"

I wasn't sure whether it would be good to pass—that is, test positive for ADHD. But I did, with flying colors. The psychologist's report confirmed severe ADHD and noted that it was likely to have caused significant impairment (and frustration).

Well, I've always been good at taking tests.

Because you're reading this book, you've likely been diagnosed. If not, it may be time to get the opinion of an experienced professional.

For suspected bipolar disorder, your best bet is a psychiatrist. Psychiatrists (unlike psychologists) can prescribe medication, which you'll almost certainly need to start if you're diagnosed as bipolar.

For suspected ADHD, start with a psychologist. Psychologists can't prescribe, but (unlike psychiatrists) they specialize in diagnostic testing.

For other mental/mood concerns, you should be fine to start with either.

This isn't to say that your family doctor, internist, or therapist can't recognize manic depression. Depending on his or her specialty, that person might even get the diagnosis right the first time. (Wouldn't that be awesome?) Ideally, though, your doctor or therapist would refer you to a specialist for confirmation and further consultation.

Don't know where to start? Try starting here for information and referrals:

NAMI HelpLine: 800-950-NAMI (6264) or info@nami.org, Monday-Friday 10 a.m.-6 p.m. EST

Also see Appendix B for a few other resources.

> According to an international study, the brains of bipolars are *literally* different from those of nonbipolars: Their gray matter is thinner, especially in the frontal and temporal regions, which control inhibition, emotion, and motivation. This difference may be one reason why manic-depressives have difficulty regulating moods. (University of Southern California)

For the many reasons discussed at the start of this chapter, doctors of all sorts often miss or misdiagnose bipolar disorder. The usual misdiagnoses include

- Major unipolar depression (60 percent)
- Anxiety disorders (26 percent)
- Schizophrenia (18 percent)
- Borderline or antisocial personality disorder (17 percent)

Researchers have found that bipolar disorder is especially likely to be mistaken for borderline personality disorder (Chapter 5). In such cases, the misdiagnosis may be discovered only *after* bipolar disorder is diagnosed and treated because then, the traits of personality disorder disappear.

Comorbidities also go into the mix. An estimated 60 to 70 percent of bipolars have ADHD, for example, and 20 percent of people with ADHD are also bipolar. But the symptoms can overlap in both the manic/hypomanic and depressive cycles of bipolar disorder, making it harder to tease these illnesses apart.

Apart from the appallingly long average wait for correct diagnosis, misdiagnosis can cause great harm. According to the National Institute of Mental Health (NIMH), an estimated 83 percent of bipolars are "seriously impaired." Can you think of any other serious illness that *isn't* diagnosed—and treated—as soon as possible?

Another problem is that doctors who mistake bipolar disorder for major depression—again, the usual misdiagnosis—often start those patients on antidepressants. Yet antidepressants can be risky; they're capable of inducing mania in up to 40 percent of undiagnosed bipolars and/or causing rapid cycling (Chapter 8).

It gets worse, because bipolar disorder extends far beyond the people who have it. Every year in the United States alone, the health-care system racks up more than $150 billion in direct and indirect costs of treating bipolar disorder. And the later bipolars are diagnosed, the larger the tab.

Can you stand even more discouraging word?

Economic

- Bipolar disorder accounts for 180 million lost workdays and $25.9 billion in lost wages every year in the United States. On average, each employee with bipolar disorder loses 49.5 workdays per year.
- A study of bipolar adults by the National Depressive and Manic-Depressive Association (NDMDA) reported that 57 percent of respondents were unemployed and that fewer than half earned a living wage.
- Only half of bipolar patients still have a job six months after psychiatric hospitalization.

Treatment

- In the first year after bipolar diagnosis, medical costs for uninsured patients average $19,000.
- A 1998 study cited average direct medical costs of $11,720 per year for patients with only one manic episode versus $624,785 per year for patients with chronic or treatment-resistant manic episodes. Can you imagine what the tab must be now?
- Forty percent of people who have bipolar disorder will receive inpatient care at least once.

Disability

- Bipolar disorder ranks sixth on the World Health Organization (WHO) list of disorders that cause disability-adjusted life-years in developed countries—a measure of the burden of disease and healthy life lost due to early death or disability.
- Compared with BP Is, BP IIs experience higher rates of disability.

Suicide*

- One-quarter to half of people with bipolar disorder attempt suicide at least once.
- The lifetime risk of suicide is higher among BP IIs than BP Is, and more BP IIs complete their attempts.

For all these reasons, it's best for anyone who exhibits clear symptoms of bipolar disorder to be assessed by a specialist, preferably one who has board certification and/or experience in treating bipolars. There's no gold standard in diagnosis, and even the best doctors can make mistakes, but those who are trained to treat bipolar patients are most likely to recognize the disorder when they see it. Training matters. You wouldn't ask a psychiatrist to take out your appendix, would you?

* Also see "The Bipolar Big Chill" in Chapter 7.

The Many manic Depressions

Four ways.

How simple and logical it would be to have only two types of bipolar disorder! Yin and yang, push and pull, 0 and 1, Twitter and civilization: the world runs on duality. But we all know that the world makes no sense, so *bipolar* is really *quadpolar*, coming in four major sizes:

- *Bipolar I*: One or more episodes of mania for at least seven days, with or without hospitalization, usually (but not necessarily) with alternating depressive episodes
- *Bipolar II*: Alternating episodes of hypomania and depression with no manic episodes
- *Cyclothymia*: Episodes of unstable moods for at least two years, with hypomania, mild depression, and short (less than eight weeks) periods of normal mood
- *Bipolar Disorder Not Otherwise Specified (NOS)*: Disorder that doesn't meet the diagnostic criteria for BP I, BP II, or cyclothymia but still features abnormal, clinically significant mood swings

As you might expect, however, these four sizes don't necessarily fit all. They may even overlap. Specific markers for BP II, for example, include cyclothymia and rapid cycling, and studies suggest that one may lead to the other. There are also several well-known types of complicated misdiagnosis. BP Is who exhibit psychotic symptoms may be mistaken for schizophrenics. BP IIs spend so much more depressed than BP Is—a ratio of 37:1* as opposed to 3:1, according to one medical journal—that they're routinely assumed to be unipolar depressives. That same journal also says that mood lability, hyperactivity, and daydreaming are markers of BP II, even though hyperactivity is *also* a marker of ADHD and despite the fact that everyone daydreams (or should do every now and then).

But wait—there's more. That "more" is the *bipolar spectrum*, which includes two additional bipolar categories:

- *Bipolar IV*: Manic/hypomaniac episodes triggered by antidepressants
- *Bipolar V*: Depression only, despite a family history of bipolar disorder

(What do you suppose happened to bipolar III? I'm barely numerate, but even I can see that when you count I, II, IV, V, something is wrong.)

Are BPs IV and V really bipolar disorder? Some experts say so. I disagree (on an amateur basis). For starters, I'm a certified BP II who was kicked into mania by an antidepressant (Chapter 6); do I have to be BP IV instead, or too? What about the people a few branches up my family tree—which likely grew some bipolars—who had only major depression? Surely they weren't ancestral BP Vs.

We're not done here. The bipolar spectrum may include nonbipolar conditions that are said to have common features, such as bulimia, anorexia, personality disorders (Chapter 5), and treatment-resistant unipolar depression (which, for the *n*th time, may well be misdiagnosed bipolar).

Not done yet. Bipolar disorder and the bipolar spectrum *themselves* may overlap, as in unipolar depression with mood swings. Drugs, alcohol, and/or medical conditions such as stroke can cause bipolary symptoms. Moreover, rapid cycling (Chapter 8) features in many of these categories.

You know what? I say it's spinach, and I say to hell with it.**

Unless your doctor is hopelessly devoted to Aristotelian taxonomy or you can't get enough granularity, maybe stick to the major categories. Manic depression is complicated enough four ways. We can safely leave all extra ways to Cincinnati chili.***

* Other studies say 40:1.
** From the 1928 *New Yorker* cartoon captioned by the immortal E.B. White.
*** This type of chili comes in up to five ways (the five being chili, spaghetti, beans, onions, and cheese), and it would be surprising if Cincinnatians haven't devised more.

What light through yonder window breaks? It is the east, but if there's any sun, it's obscured by foggy language. Would you call the east a soft west or the sun a soft black hole? Certainly not. That would be crazy. You can bet Shakespeare wouldn't have. So why do so many theoretically sane non-Elizabethans call bipolar II "soft" bipolar?

But Soft . . .

Every BP II knows better. BP I is more dramatic, with all that exciting mania and sexy misbehavior, but it's not worse. Statistically, BP II is. A study that compared bipolars of both types found that BP IIs are symptomatic 55.8 percent of the time, whereas BP Is display symptoms 9.2 percent less often (46.6 percent of the time).

Moreover, other studies have found that BP IIs

- Attempt and successfully commit suicide at greater rates
- Are more prone to rapid cycling and comorbidities
- Experience more severe, longer-lasting depression with greater impairment
- Have shorter well periods between hypomanic and depressive cycles

This isn't soft. It's hard-core. If people try to tell you otherwise, feel free to thwack them on the head with a copy of this book or a croquet mallet.

What did we do before the Internet? Here's what we didn't: doctor ourselves. If we're smart, we don't now. Bipolars already tend toward hypochondria, so the medical Internet can be virtual crack for us.

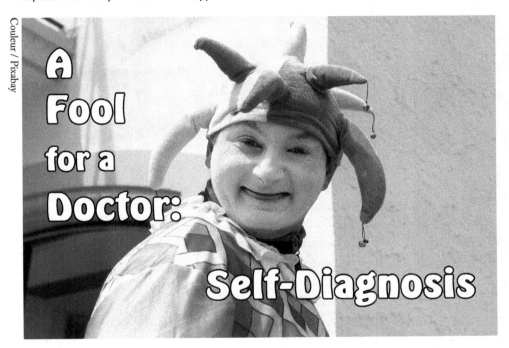

Couleur / Pixabay

A Fool for a Doctor: Self-Diagnosis

Think about it. There are online quizzes for everything, and I'll bet you a double-shot iced vanilla latte that you've taken one to see whether you have bipolar disorder, even if a psychiatrist has already confirmed it. How did you do?

C'mon, get real; you'd have come out the same if you'd flipped a coin. Just because a website diagnosed bipolar disorder doesn't mean it's right when it says you *also* have diverticulitis, or Lyme disease, or that thing that makes people think they turn into wolves at the full moon. (Lycanthropy.)

In fairness, though, I admit to committing self-diagnosis. You could ask Dr. J. Every winter, I get respiratory infections but wait too long to see him because I *know* what's wrong, what with being a board-certified, bottled-in-bond, infallible master physician who doesn't need doctors. —Kidding. My internist is a fine doctor with real board certification and an acute sense of humor. Dr. J. knows how it is with me and listens gravely to my diagnoses for about 60 seconds before dropping the hammer. (Later, we laugh.)

Don't do this. I'm trying to stop it myself. Let your M.D. figure out what ails your body, and call your psychologist or psychiatrist when your head is a mess. You don't think they diagnose *themselves* on Playbuzz, do you?

> **Full disclosure #1:** While writing this chapter, I took a werewolf quiz online. You'll never guess: I *am* a werewolf. Take that, you bipolar creatures of the night!

You and I are not alone in this bipolar situation. Following are a few of the many famous people who have (or had, or are thought to have had) bipolar disorder. We stand in illustrious company.

Meet the Family

Stephen Fry
Mel Gibson
Gerry Goffin
Halsey
Linda Hamilton
Mariette Hartley
Ernest Hemingway
Jimi Hendrix
Margot Kidder
Vivien Leigh
Demi Lovato
Sir Isaac Newton
Sinead O'Connor

Jane Pauley
Frank Sinatra
Britney Spears
Leo Tolstoy
Ted Turner
Jean-Claude Van Damme
Vincent Van Gogh
Kanye West
Brian Wilson
Amy Winehouse
Catherine Zeta-Jones

Ludwig von Beethoven
Russell Brand
Mariah Carey
Kurt Cobain

Patty Duke
Brian Epstein
Carrie Fisher
Zelda Fitzgerald

Many lists of famous bipolars include Winston Churchill, but the International Churchill Society says that's bollocks. —No, it didn't. The good people at the society would never say that. They *do* say it's only a myth (Chapter 7). Same goes for Lindsay Lohan, who reportedly was misdiagnosed a few years back.

That said, there's still some question as to whether Zelda Fitzgerald was bipolar, schizophrenic, or both. (You can *be* both if you're extremely unlucky.) Her doctors thought she was schizophrenic because of her psychotic symptoms, but psychosis can occur in severe bipolar I mania. My money would be on BP I. Our bipolar kinsman Ernest Hemingway wrote about her and Scott at length in *A Moveable Feast*; his brilliant, chilling portrait comes into focus most clearly when you see her through a BP I lens. I include her here on the authority of Mr. Hemingway (and because I've always loved that book); we'll never know for sure.

Loony Toons?

Just for fun, can you think of cartoon characters who'd be bipolar if they were real? Most of them *could* be, which is one reason to watch cartoons even now. Here's my short list:

Bugs Bunny in *The Rabbit of Seville*   Sylvester the Cat
Wile E. Coyote   Yosemite Sam
Daffy Duck   Most Groucho Marx characters
Donald Duck   Every last one of the Three Stooges

I realize that not all of the above are animations. Don't overthink this.

Looney Tunes characters dominate the list because they tend to be on the deranged side, which is what you want in cartoons. I went back and forth on Michigan J. Frog, whose two speeds are Inert and Super Freak. And Tweety Bird is nowhere near normal. But you can't say that Tweety is bipolar, exactly—maybe a wee touch psycho. (By the way, my mom loved him.)

Looney Tunes end card, Warner Bros. / public domain

What @#&^%!! Else Could Go Wrong?

Chapter 5

Y ou'd think that having bipolar disorder would be bother enough, and it is. But this is no perfect world, with perfect mathematical distribution of inconvenience; in this world, 1 = 2, 3, or more. Here's proof: Researchers have found that two-thirds of bipolars have at least one other psychiatric condition.

The technical name for this outrage is *comorbid*. Merriam-Webster says it means "existing simultaneously with and usually independently of another medical condition." Having a black sense of humor, I like this word better than *co-occurring*, but you can use the second one if you prefer.

> "It's not a mental illness, but high sensitivity often tailgates on manic depression. Because of how we're wired, many bipolars are also highly sensitive, particularly to noise and other environmental stimuli. Too much overstimulation can overwhelm us, possibly triggering a manic/hypomanic or depressive episode. (*Psychology Today* online)"

In addition to bipolar II, for example, I carry around ADHD (inattentive type), anxiety, mostly silent migraines, and a few allergies. Your load may vary (see "Not to Be Comorbid, But . . ." in this chapter). Only the ADHD comorbidity is severe, but five (*five!*) diagnoses is a heavy lift some days.

As everyone knows, or should know, prescription and over-the-counter (OTC) meds may disagree. Also, one condition can make another worse. In addition, it can be difficult—and stressful—to decide whether you're physically ill or having a bipolar event, and stress weakens the immune system something awful.

Medical troubles are nuisances by themselves; trying to manage them while bipolar is exponentially worse, adding insult to fairly regular injury. You might say that our comorbidities are comorbid with our comorbidities.

This is no fun.

The best we can probably do is keep our doctors' numbers on speed dial and make sure that all of them have the other doctors' numbers. Bipolar disorder is a lifelong condition that tends to keep bad company; take your health seriously by calling the appropriate specialist when you feel less than right.

(For the record, if a deathless love of '80s New Wave counts as a comorbidity, I've got that one too.)

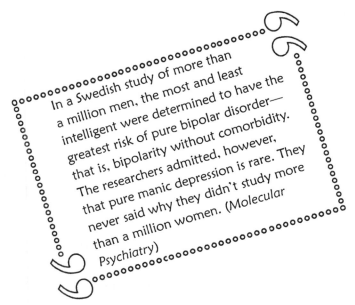

> "In a Swedish study of more than a million men, the most and least intelligent were determined to have the greatest risk of pure bipolar disorder—that is, bipolarity without comorbidity. The researchers admitted, however, that pure manic depression is rare. They never said why they didn't study more than a million women. (*Molecular Psychiatry*)"

One of the more unpleasant facts of having a major psychiatric diagnosis is that if you have one, you probably have more. A recent study found that 65 percent of bipolars have at least one other disorder. Here are a few:

Not to Be Comorbid, But . . .

- *ADHD*: Not just for children. The two types are inattentive and hyperactive-impulsive, but some people have both. If you have bipolar disorder of any variety, you're likely to have ADHD too; an estimated 70 percent of bipolars do. (See "Fish! Sunglasses! Mad Men!" in this chapter to find out what ADHD feels like.)
- *Anxiety disorders*: Not just everyday worry. The kinds that get doctors involved include obsessive-compulsive disorder, panic disorder, and some phobias. BP IIs, incidentally, are more likely to develop anxiety disorders than BP Is are.
- *Substance use disorders (SUDs)*: Diagnosed in an estimated 48 percent of bipolar II patients (and a whopping 61 percent of those with bipolar I).* The leading SUD is alcohol abuse; misuse of prescription and street drugs is close behind.
- *Obsessive-compulsive disorder (OCD)*: A chronic mental illness manifested by obsessive thoughts and repetitive behaviors. One study found that bipolars have an 18-fold greater risk of developing OCD than the general population.
- *Personality disorders*: Psychological disorders characterized by persistent thoughts and behavior that impair normal functioning. ("What Characters!" in this chapter discusses personality disorders.)
- *Medical illnesses*: Generally speaking, whatever you'd see your internist or family doctor for. According to a study cited in *The British Journal of Psychiatry*, the most common medical comorbidities with BP II are

    o Migraines (23.7 percent)
    o Asthma (19.2 percent)
    o Elevated lipids, which means high cholesterol and triglycerides in the bloodstream (also 19.2 percent)
    o Hypertension (16.8 percent)

The journal further says that the rates of gastric ulcers, heart disease, Parkinson's disease, and rheumatoid arthritis are significantly higher among BP IIs.

---

* SUDs occur so often in people with mental illnesses of all kinds that the combination is called a *dual diagnosis*.

L to R (all Pixabay): dina263 (goldfish), michael-kouassi (plus signs), and Clker-Free-Vector-Images (sunglasses and whiskey)

Fish! Sunglasses! Mad Men!

The ADHD Experience

These three things have nothing in common except in an ADHD brain, which might connect them this way: "Fish live in water; and people wear sunglasses at the beach, which is next to water; and you know who looks good in sunglasses? The guy on *Mad Men*. Don Draper. I mean, Jon Hamm. Wasn't he a trip on *30 Rock*? Hey, my brother knows Liz Lemon! I mean, Tina Fey. Should we have another macchiato? Because I feel like I'm rambling here, and caffeine is good for focus. Something else that's good for you is fish, if you like it. You know, fish live in water. Did I mention that there was a lot of swimming on *Mad Men*? Did you see Don Draper on *30 Rock*? Hey, where are you going?"

At this point, whoever you're with has remembered an urgent reason not to be. You're in the wrong company. You need to hang with someone more like you. Then you can order flat whites and talk till they close the Starbucks.

So true. Several friends may have at least a touch of ADHD because they talk like I do when I'm off the meds. By way of example, I've spent many happy summer nights drinking Chardonnay on a friend's front porch until the wee smalls, both of us talking about absolutely everything *at the same time* but still understanding *every single word* the other one said.

> Much of Don Draper's swimming on *Mad Men* took place during Season 4, starting with "The Summer Man" (Episode 8). There was also that incident in "A Tale of Two Cities" (Season 6, Episode 10) in which he smoked hash at a party in LA and wound up face-down in the pool. Roger Sterling saved him. You could look it up.

This ability is a signature function of ADHD. If you're like me and these friends of mine, you "hear" conversations several sentences ahead, and because you've already "heard" a thing you want to respond to, you skip the stuff in between. You interrupt a lot without meaning to, or even realizing *that* you do, because you're already where the other person is going. You think fast, talk fast, process faster. So it's a pleasure to hang with someone who thinks, talks, and processes the way you do—someone who really *gets* you. This is why you can spend long summer nights sharing bottles of wine with someone you're not out to sleep with. This person might be a soulmate without sex, I guess, or a brother from a different mother, or a sister from a different mister.

(I made the last one up, but it kind of works, doesn't it? Did I mention that there was a lot of swimming on *Mad Men*?)

Another way to understand the ADHD experience is to picture a pinball machine. When you're up and running, your brain is an arcade. It's bright shiny moving things, flashing lights, bells, and music all going at the same time, and you don't need a quarter to play.

Or picture the midway at any county fair. The rides are lit up like pinball, but the music is louder (also heavier on calliope), and on top of that, every sense gets triggered:

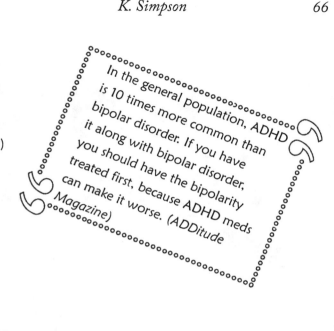

In the general population, ADHD is 10 times more common than bipolar disorder. If you have it along with bipolar disorder, you should have the bipolarity treated first, because ADHD meds can make it worse. (ADDitude Magazine)

- While you're trying hard to decide which ride to ride first, you **hear** the corn-dog tent calling your name, so you go there.
- You're already eating an elephant ear because it **tastes** good and you can.
- Back on the midway, you **smell** the crowd in line for the Ferris wheel, which is a revolting thing to smell on such a hot night.
- You've bought a ticket for the Ferris wheel anyway when you **see** the Octopus, which is more fun, so you go there.
- The Octopus upsets your stomach because you had all those corn dogs, and the cracked leatherette seat **feels** sticky on your shorts. Gross!

That's all five, right? Add the sense of shame for spending so much money trying to win a goldfish in a bowl, and we've pretty well covered it.

—Wasn't I trying to make a point here? I started to, but R.E.M. is playing, and I was singing along and got sidetracked. Did you know I can sing and write at the same time? It's harder to do with R.E.M. because of all the lyrics, but—

Never mind. The point (I think) is that as confusing as ADHD may be to everyone else, it's more confusing for those of us who have it. The world is full of distractions, and we're wired to like—and chase—all of them at the same time. That's hard on focus. Caffeine helps. But Adderall helps better (Chapter 9).

By the way, I loved *Mad Men*, which *did* have a lot of swimming. Lots of sunglasses too. Not many fish.

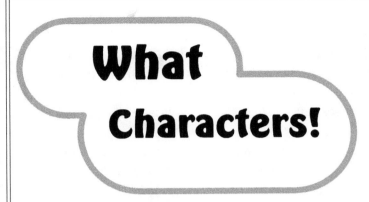

What Characters!

You're probably familiar with Freud's three-part theory of personality: id, ego, and superego. And you've known people whose parts are unpleasantly out of balance, if not downright out of whack. Personality disorders,* however, are unpleasant *and* unbalanced. They're nonmedical mental problems characterized by persistent, unhealthy thought patterns and at least one pathological personality trait, and they significantly impair everyday life.

Many online tests purport to reveal personality disorders, but *DSM-5* (Chapter 4) has specific diagnostic requirements, including stability over time and across situations. And the behavior must be abnormal for the person's environment and developmental stage, with no direct effect from drugs, alcohol, or other medical conditions.

The manual lists ten personality disorders, grouped in three categories:

Cluster A (odd, bizarre, eccentric)	Cluster B (dramatic, erratic)	Cluster C (anxious, fearful)
Paranoid	Antisocial	Avoidant
Schizoid	Borderline	Dependent
Schizotypal	Histrionic	Obsessive-compulsive**
	Narcissistic	

Descriptions of these disorders are beyond the scope of this book. But be aware that the categories aren't carved in stone: Many people who have one personality disorder have another, and disorders in each category may overlap.

Unlike most other mental illnesses, personality disorders aren't treated with medication; in fact, the U.S. Food and Drug Administration (FDA) hasn't approved any drug for that purpose. Treatment generally involves outpatient psychotherapy of some kind (unless the symptoms are severe enough to call for hospitalization), but doctors may prescribe antidepressants or mood stabilizers to relieve symptoms.

Despite what may be unbearable temptation, don't assume that every egomaniac you know is personality-disordered. The same goes for drama queens of all genders, garden-variety conspiracy theorists, and oddballs in the office, not to mention people you just plain don't like. A vile or annoying personality isn't always disordered, so it's no fair to call out vile or annoying people as such.

If they're *also* appalling swine, however, have at them. Just make sure to call them out only as pork

---

* Also called *character disorders.*

** Similar but not identical to obsessive-compulsive anxiety disorder.

These are a few things I've learned the hard way about managing bipolar II and medical comorbidities.

Check interactions on all your medications—prescription and OTC—for all your situations.

Your doctor's office should have detailed medical records and shouldn't prescribe meds that clash with others. Also, most pharmacies run automatic interaction checks whenever you fill a new prescription. But these safeguards won't work properly if you don't tell your doctor about all the meds you take (legal and otherwise) or don't get all your prescriptions filled at the same pharmacy.

Before you start any new medication, make certain that you know how well it plays with your bipolar *and* your OTC meds. Also ask about concomitant caffeine, alcohol, and tobacco use, which you should do anyway (Chapter 9).

Don't diagnose yourself. Really, don't.

Medical apps and websites are fine for casual research. Try that, but stop there: These apps and sites can make hypochondriacs of us all. See Chapter 4 for reasons to avoid do-it-yourself diagnosis.

Managing Medical Multiples

See an M.D. when you need to.

Bipolar disorder is enough to make anyone sick; anything acute on top of it calls for professional care. See your physician, internist, or nurse practitioner when you're physically ill. Get a second opinion if you want and a third if you must. But get opinions only from people who went to med school (or—if *you* went to med school—from someone else who went).

Take your medication.

What a concept! I only recently figured out that taking medicine works better than leaving it in a kitchen cabinet (behind the allergy pills and antacids). Turns out that you can't skip bipolar medication without getting into trouble, and taking any other drugs your doctor prescribes might possibly help some too.

But don't take all meds.

The preceding rule doesn't apply to every drug. That includes herbals, even though I have friends who swear by them; K. grows many of her own herbs, takes complicated potions of them, and says they work like a charm. Maybe so. Maybe no. Check with your doctor, though. St. John's wort, for example, doesn't like Prozac *at all*, and vice versa. Take them together, and you run the risk of a severe reaction called serotonin syndrome, which I've experienced myself (Chapter 9) and wouldn't wish on anyone.

Almost anyone.

Then there's that other herb, now legal in some states; I swore by that one myself many years ago. Legal or not, though, it's something you probably have no business using if you take bipolar meds. The same goes for street drugs. You know this, don't you?

Part 3

Up / Down / Both

Chapter 6

Up

A little Dalíance.

Hypomania is the good part. Not always the nice part. Sometimes, it's a rat gnawing on your brain; sometimes, it's a rat dragging pizza through it.* These are not attractive metaphors. But during hypomania, *something* is running on a wheel in your head, squeaking with excitement and whipping its tail. It's bigger than a mouse, more dangerous than a gerbil, smarter than a hamster. So I say it's a rat.

I also still say it's the good part. I *like* hypomania.

Twenty-odd years ago, after my last hospitalization, a psychiatrist prescribed Wellbutrin—a pill the color of sunshine, which was cheering. Then it got *really* cheering. How much? Well, an uncle died a few weeks later, and I was the life of the party at his wake and funeral— inappropriate, but 180 from the way I'd felt in the hospital. Now I was wired, wisecracking, even giddy. This behavior lasted a couple of weeks, along with more uncoordination than usual.

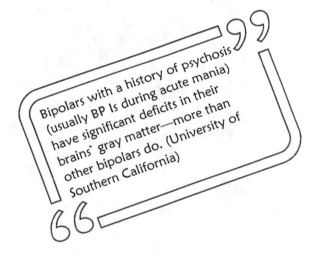

Bipolars with a history of psychosis (usually BP Is during acute mania) have significant deficits in their brains' gray matter—more than other bipolars do. (University of Southern California)

I almost didn't mention the last part to the psychiatrist at our next session and have often wished I hadn't. This doctor was no fun; he stopped the magic yellow pill and substituted an SSRI that didn't work. *Or* feel good.

This episode may have been mania. That it seems to have been medication-induced is a detail: I displayed six of the seven *DSM-5* criteria for mania from section B and the duration from section A. That week or two was a bullet-train ride and a blast; even that funeral felt like a party.

I *did* tell the psychiatrist about the last part. Even I was starting to think that fun at a funeral might be a little off.

There've been no episodes that extreme in the years since (and no more manic reactions to Wellbutrin), but there've been many cycles of what I now know is hypomania. For me, the main difference between that and mania is a lower high. During hypomania, I still have ill-advised spending sprees, flights of ideas, secret (and not-so-secret) grandiosity, and little interest in food or sleep. My mood is good except for random bursts of irritability. I multitask like a caffeinated octopus. Like most BP IIs, I live for hypomanic cycles, which almost make up for the depressive ones. And I cram as much living as possible into hypomania because it never lasts.

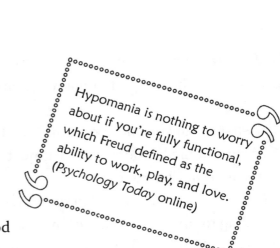

Hypomania is nothing to worry about if you're fully functional, which Freud defined as the ability to work, play, and love. (*Psychology Today* online)

Medication helps even out the cycles, of course. Dr. M. said the med he prescribed would give me a floor and a ceiling, which was true even during the long, slow titration phase. But I'll continue to go high and low. The only big change should be fewer extremes.

This is fine.

A British study found that antidepressant treatment increases the risk of manic episodes by 6 percent, particularly for patients who take SSRIs. (*BMJ Open*)

Both BP Is and BP IIs can experience hypomanic (and manic) episodes, but the course tends to be different in BP II. More often than not, BP II hypomania manifests itself as irritability rather than hyperactivity. A fellow BP II said it all on PsychCentral: "Nobody understands people with bipolar II because there's no high; there's just anger and angst."**

Well, yes and no. I *have* highs, as it happens, but also whole hypomanic cycles of being nothing but snappish and agitated, and irritation can break through an otherwise-larky mood with no warning. A few months ago, during a high cycle, I dropped a small tool and went from fine to absolutely furious justlikethat. So I picked up the tool and threw it as hard and as fast and as far as I could. (Disappointingly, nothing broke.)

I'd like to tell you that this sort of thing almost never happens, but now that I'm aware that it does, I have to admit that it's part of many hypomanic episodes.

So what can anyone do about this? You'll find a discussion of current medications and treatments for hypomania (and mania) in Chapter 9.

"Hypomanic cycles are often triggered by seasonal changes, especially in the spring, when days start getting longer and sunlight begins to increase."

Treatment is controversial in some quarters, though. According to the World Federation of Societies of Biological Psychiatry, BP II hypomania needs no separate therapy. To minimize the risk of escalation to full-blown mania, it says, the doctor may simply want to put the patient on an antipsychotic for a short time.

The line between mania and hypomania can be thin, however. The line between an extreme manic episode and a psychotic break can be hairline. Your safest bet is to know the warning signs (see "Maniac, Maniac on the Floor" in this chapter) and make sure that someone close to you knows them too. You may not always know when you're in hypomania, but if you have bipolar disorder, you absolutely *will* go there, so it's good for someone to keep a watchful (but friendly) eye out.

With luck, you'll never go higher than you can safely fly. But we bipolars should never trust to luck alone.

---

* Look up *pizza rat* in your favorite search engine.

** From "Bipolar II: Anger, Angst & Understanding," by Candy Czernicki, https://psychcentral.com/blog/bipolar-ii-anger-angst-understanding, accessed July 19, 2019. Reprinted with permission.

If you're curious what extreme manic depression looks like, you might check out *Wolf Hall*, the 2015 BBC miniseries. It's not only perfectly cast and staged, but also a textbook portrait of a worst-case bipolar scenario. Historians don't believe that the real Henry VIII was manic-depressive; severe head injuries during jousts and, later, dementia are thought to have scrambled his eggs. But the Henry in this miniseries and the Hilary Mantel novels is a BP I if ever there was one, probably also psychotic, without doubt a giant sexist murderous egomaniacal impotent (they say) pig.

jplenio / Pixabay

Telling a hypomanic cycle from an ordinary good mood and mania from hypomania can be tricky, especially from the inside. But knowledgeable observers can pick up on telltale signs. Three or more of the following symptoms may signal a manic or hypomanic episode:

- Abnormal upbeat mood
- Increase in activity, energy, or agitation
- Exaggerated well-being and self-confidence (euphoria)
- Less need for sleep

- More talkativeness
- Racing thoughts (flights of ideas)
- Distractibility
- Poor and/or risky decision-making

How can anyone tell the difference? Maybe they can't. Generally, though, mania is worse than hypomania, often derailing relationships and ordinary life. When severe enough, it could trigger a psychotic break that requires a stay in the hospital. For these reasons alone, the symptoms need watching.

DSM-5 criteria say that a manic episode lasts a week or more and that hypomania lasts at least four days; in both cases, symptoms are present for most of the day nearly every day. Further, the manual says that the symptoms in both types of episodes are distinct, abnormal, and persistent.

Finally, as for the differences between these episodes in bipolar I and II:

- *BP I*: Hypomania is common in this form of the disorder but not definitive. Psychotic symptoms, however, *are* definitive.
- *BP II*: At least one hypomanic and one depressive episode (past or present) define bipolar II.

Keep an eye on yourself as best you can during a hypomanic cycle; ask the people closest to you to do the same. Chapter 12 suggests ways that loved ones and others can help.

Maniac, Maniac on the Floor

True mania tends to be up front, out loud, and in your face. It's hard to miss. It's a defining feature of BP I but can strike bipolars of any stripe, especially when they take certain antidepressants (Chapter 9).

Not every manic episode is like every other manic episode, but some combination of the following symptoms is common:

- Loud, rapid-fire, and/or nonstop talking
- Flight of ideas, often expressed in disorganized, incoherent speech
- Decreased need for sleep
- Exaggerated self-esteem, grandiosity, and/or narcissistic delusions
- Irritability and agitation
- Reckless indulgences such as spending sprees, daredevil driving, and sexual promiscuity
- Extreme multitasking
- Unusual sociability, to the point of obnoxiousness
- Trouble sitting still or concentrating

In severe cases, mania tips into *psychosis*: delusions, hallucinations, false beliefs, and similar departures from everyday reality. During a psychotic break, a person may see and hear things that don't exist, which may trigger paranoia. Severe psychosis almost always calls for hospitalization and medication.

Speaking of medication, all too often, BP Is skip doses or stop their meds altogether. The high of mania feels so good that it's hard to resist feeling it again. This is a good reason for friends, family members, and other close associates to keep sharp watch on bipolars who seemed to be stable and suddenly don't.

A Swiss study suggests that mania gives off subtle warning signs during the *prodrome* (a period of up to 21 weeks before the episode occurs), including changed sleep patterns, mood lability, functional impairment, and problems with concentration. Still, in bipolar disorder, cycles may come and go without warning, so there may be no sign—subtle or otherwise—during the prodrome.

Mania Lightish

Hypomania is sometimes called *mania light*, but *mania lightish* is more accurate. This type of episode, which characterizes BP II, has the same symptoms as full-blown mania but differs in two important ways:

- Hypomania is less severe, with little impairment.
- Hypomania never includes psychotic symptoms.

The *DSM-5* (Chapter 4) defines hypomania as a clearly elevated, expansive, or irritable mood that persists for at least four consecutive days and for most of those days; mania is similar but lasts a week or more.

Being a BP II, I'm an experienced hypomaniac and have to say I like it. The cycle is shorter than the depressive one but can last for months, and for me, every minute is a pleasure (except when it's not; see Chapter 1). It may wreck sleep, screw with concentration, and amp up attitude, but mostly, hypomania is good.

This is bad.

Fine as it feels, hypomania is a bipolar cycle. When revved up to the max, it can look, act, and feel a lot like mania, and BP IIs have been known to tip into the full-blown kind. This phenomenon is usually drug-induced (as described at the start of this chapter), but not always.

For that reason, it's a good idea to ask a trusted friend or relative to intervene if/when a hypomanic cycle seems more extreme than usual. In severe mania *or* hypomania, you could endanger yourself and others, and no temporary high is worth that risk.

Chapter 7

Down

What goes up, of course, comes down. Sir Isaac Newton said so; BP IIs know so. We're down far more than up, and in ways all our own. A BP I might crash for a week or two, whereas a BP II might stay crashed for months . . . or years. Because we're wired to take things harder, it takes us longer to get back up when we're knocked down.

My own depressions started during high school, which is typical of bipolar II. For many years, these depressions were misdiagnosed as unipolar, so I was treated (and hospitalized) as such. This, too, is typical. And early on, I came thisclose to suicide. Also typical.

In *An Unquiet Mind*, Dr. Kay Jamison recalled that her mind had been once her best friend. As the good doctor must have been when she wrote that line, I'm darkly amused by the irony. My own best friend started turning on me when I was 13, and though we're still on cordial terms, it turns on me to this day. Mostly to depression.

> Depression is the leading cause of disability worldwide, with 6.9 percent of adults experiencing major depression. (NAMI)

Every depressive episode is different, if only minutely. Some episodes are clearly related to loss, disappointment, or upsetting events. Some appear to come out of nowhere. Some lift a bit in response to positive events. Some don't budge. And some have mixed features, confusing everyone.

I've experienced all these kinds and more. My depressions tend to be atypical (see "Sinking Outside the Box" in this chapter) and recurring. They're usually worst in winter (comorbid with respiratory infections), but in my 20s and 30s, the opposite was true: All my hospitalizations were summer ones. Even during summer depressions, though, I hibernate. What with having a comfortable couch and a large media library, I can spend hours barely moving—the photo negative of normal. As long as the movies, caffeine, and ice cream hold out, I won't leave the house.

There've been other episodes too, bad ones, some crossed with hypomania. Those are the ones to watch. It's risky enough to think about suicide (more in the sense of "I want the pain to stop" than "I want to make myself dead") when you're too sad, tired, and slowed-down to get off the couch to commit it. It's much more dangerous to think about suicide when you're irritable and energetic, because thought can turn to deed when you're hurting enough and have the will.

> Bipolars may experience short episodes of depression before the onset of a severe depressive cycle. Early warning signs include fatigue and insomnia. (WebMD)

It can happen in a flash. That's how it happened for me. I was 19, fresh from flunking out of college (again), left alone to work a summer job while the family was away on vacation. I was also alone with a vial of my father's Seconals. Suddenly one afternoon, it occurred to me to die.

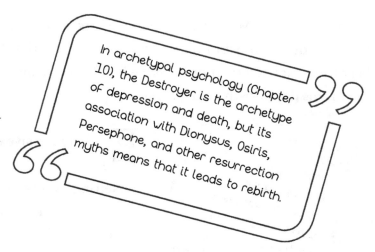

In archetypal psychology (Chapter 10), the Destroyer is the archetype of depression and death, but its association with Dionysus, Osiris, Persephone, and other resurrection myths means that it leads to rebirth.

I have a 360-degree, Technicolor memory of sitting on the hardwood floor of my bedroom in a patch of sunshine, staring at those shiny red pills, wondering how many to take. I'd already written the note. I'd already started the bourbon. For an hour or so, it was touch and go, taking pills out of the vial, putting them back, taking them out, putting them back. It was a long hour.

Even now, I don't know what triggered it. Most days that summer were bad ones, and I was already depressed enough about being left on my own in a haunted house. (Word of honor: It was.) I was also agitated about being left, period. That afternoon, I had the motive, means, energy, and will to kill myself; things might easily have gone the other way.

I don't know why they didn't.

(For the record, the black comedy of turning myself into a ghost in a haunted house never crossed my mind.)

Whatever the reason, I never got that close to suicide again. Maybe between the undiagnosed manic depression and ADHD, I couldn't decide how to do it. Or Dorothy Parker may have intervened. I read her a lot back then and still have her "Résumé" by heart: After listing the drawbacks of various sorts of self-murder, she concluded, "You might as well live."

You really might as well. There's this about being bipolar: The cycles never last.

Bipolar depression *is* quite unlike the unipolar kind. Among other things, it's more severe and feels worse. For me, it's a black cloud that hangs over everything for weeks or months—bad mental weather that drives me to hibernate, isolate, despair, and do other destructive things that I suggest *you* not do (see "Walking the Black Dog" in this chapter). This experience is pretty much status quo. Several journal articles call out a few symptoms of bipolar depression (as opposed to the unipolar kind):

Bipolar	**Unipolar**
Sudden onset	Gradual onset
Often unrelated to negative events	Often related to negative events
At least one manic/hypomanic episode	No history of mania/hypomania
Atypical symptoms*	Typical symptoms
Frequent and recurring	Seldom, if ever, recurring
Unresponsive to antidepressants	Responsive to antidepressants
Family history of bipolar disorder	No family history of bipolar disorder
Psychotic features**	No evidence of psychosis

Those who go undiagnosed may be given antidepressants (Chapter 9), which may or may not help, let alone be benign in bipolar circumstances. BP IIs in particular may be likely to get these meds, given the depth, length, and severity of their depressive cycles. Most experts, however, suggest first-line treatment with a mood stabilizer, with an antidepressant added as needed for short periods.

Whatever the treatment, two things are sure about bipolar depression: It doesn't go away on its own, and it'll be back. Treat it with care. But treat it.

---

* See "Sinking Outside the Box" in this chapter for more on atypical depression.

** Not all depressed bipolars experience psychosis, of course. More of those who do are BP I than BP II.

Unlike mania and hypomania (Chapter 6), depression is familiar to most people and for the most part easy to recognize. Bipolar depression is a somewhat different animal, however, and may require different treatment.

Here are some of the symptoms of major depression in bipolar disorder:

- Sadness and/or hopelessness
- Unusual fatigue that's not relieved by rest
- Excessive guilt
- Weight and/or appetite loss or gain
- Significantly more or less sleep
- Trouble concentrating and making decisions
- Agitated or slowed-down behavior
- Loss of interest in enjoyable activities
- Suicidal thoughts or plans

To qualify as major depression, five or more of these symptoms must be present for at least two weeks.

Bipolar depression has additional characteristic features, including rapid cycling and/or mixed states (Chapter 8).

As in nonbipolar depression, however, a depressive episode may take atypical shape. (See "Sinking Outside the Box" in this chapter.)

The movies and TV like to portray depression as a nonstop fiesta of pain: weeping, wailing, walking the floors, tearing hair, gnashing teeth, generally acting out (and up). This sounds right. It seems right. It must *be* right. Right?

Not necessarily. I like to call these depictions "Hollywood depression" because they aren't quite true. Also, there's such a thing as atypical depression, and bipolars are more likely than others to have it.

Vive some of *les différences*:

Sinking Outside the Box

Typical/Hollywood	Atypical
Depression worst in the morning	Depression worst at night
Consistent down mood	Temporary improvement in response to positive events
Loss of appetite and/or weight loss	Increased appetite and/or weight gain
Insomnia or short sleep	Increased sleep
Agitation and increased movement	Slow, heavy movement
Tends to begin in adulthood	Tends to begin in adolescence
Generally short-term	Often long-term

(By the way, it's possible to have symptoms from Column A *and* symptoms from Column B. I do.)

Atypical depression is more likely than the typical kind to feature comorbid mental illness (Chapter 5) and alcohol/drug abuse. It can also complicate relationships, because those who have this form of depression—especially BP IIs—are extra-sensitive to rejection or criticism, real or perceived.

Scientists aren't sure what causes atypical depression. Brain chemistry, history, and heredity may all play a role, especially for manic-depressives. Risk factors include

- Personal or family history of bipolar disorder
- Personal or family history of substance abuse
- Past or current stressful events (including childhood trauma)

You may think, logically enough, that atypical depression is treated with atypical antidepressants, and in some cases, it is. But so many antidepressants are available today that your doctor may have other ideas.* Chapter 9 gives you an overview of the options.

---

* Ignore the ads that tell you to "Ask your doctor" for a specific drug, because they really mean "Badger your doctor till you get a scrip for this superexpensive new shiz." Better let your doctor—presumably a trained professional—decide what to prescribe, at least at first. Psychiatric drugs aren't Pez and are not to be trifled with. Newer drugs aren't necessarily better drugs. And no one should *ever* take medical advice from a commercial.

Walking the Black Dog

If you're a person of a certain vintage, this title may flash you back to *Led Zeppelin IV*, which you'll have had on vinyl or eight-track in 1971. "Black Dog" is the first cut on side 1. But I'm thinking here of Winston Churchill, who made frequent references to his "black dog" and was said to suffer severe bipolar depression.

That last part may be nonsense. The International Churchill Society's website says so. It also says he said, "I do believe I am a glow-worm." (Really.)

Worm or not, Churchill *did* talk a lot about this dog, which is still a perfectly useful metaphor. So let's pretend we don't know that the story is bogus.

How, then, do you walk a black dog? By this, I mean how do you keep yourself away from the squirrels and out of traffic when you're bipolarly depressed?

You may not be able to do much about the squirrels in your life; we all have them. But you can do a few things to make yourself calmer, more comfortable, and less likely to sink deeper while you're down. BP IIs go deep enough.

Try these.

(**Note:** Not all of the following suggestions may apply to those who live with other people. For the view from the other side, see Chapter 12.)

Try to follow a routine.

The more predictable your day is, the less likely you are to be stirred and shaken by surprises. If you can safely go to work, go. If you can't (or if you're on medical leave or not working), at least try getting up and turning in at regular times. Psychiatric hospitals keep patients on a schedule (Chapter 3) because structure helps; even a minimal homemade routine may help you too.

Keep taking your meds.

Don't stop taking them because you don't feel like it or don't think there's any point now. Call your doctor if you're having trouble with your meds, but don't quit them cold. Some antidepressants cause genuinely dangerous withdrawal if they're not tapered (Chapter 9), and you don't need that problem on top of the other one.

Make an effort to take care of yourself.

Self-maintenance may be the last thing you want to do while depressed, but take your best shot. Even if you're not up to lacing up your Nikes and hitting the track, a short walk, even indoors, will do you good by getting your blood circulating and oxygen flowing. (Did you know that your blood actually kludges up when you get too much bed rest—or couch rest?)

If your depression is atypical (see "Sinking Outside the Box" in this chapter), you may be getting your share of food and sleep *and* a few other people's, in which case try to moderate a little. Also get some exercise if you can. You'll feel less guilty about that bag of chocolate-covered peanuts you snarfed down while watching HGTV.

Clean up your act.

I hope that you're in the habit of showering or bathing every day. If you're able to go to work, you'll probably stick to that habit, if only minimally. When you're full-time depressed at home, however, there may come days when you decide that you can't be bothered. *Bother.* You may be surprised how much better a little soap and shampoo can make you feel. The same goes for clean day clothes and/or nightwear.

Besides, unless you're all hyenas, those around you will appreciate a little hygiene.

(Feel free to skip beard maintenance, mascara, and/or hair product till you're out of the woods.)

When at home, try not to isolate.

Many depressed bipolars want to go to bed, pull the covers over their head, and stay there till Hell freezes or the mood lifts, whichever comes first. And why not? No one feels like socializing at times like these. But you can still be sort of social from home, so try texting or e-mailing a friend once in a while. Or—here's a wacky idea—phone someone. Who doesn't like getting a call that's *not* from a spambot?

However you reach out, whoever you touch, human contact matters. People who need people—and that's all of them—need people most when they're depressed.

When at work, don't oversocialize.

Your job (if you're working) probably involves at least some forced socialization, in which case you *can't* isolate. This is OK. You can go through the motions for a while. Besides, unless you're Meryl Streep, everyone already knows you're depressed and will probably cut you some slack. Take a little.

Be polite if you can't be nice. Do your job and *only* your job. Skip lunch with the gang if you're not up to it. Pass up the many birthday-cake extravaganzas in the break room if you're not up to them. Turn down drinks after work (and you really shouldn't be drinking on psychiatric meds anyway). Try not to be rude, though; you still have to work with your co-workers.

If things get *too* bad, talk to HR about medical leave (Chapter 11). Then stay in bed all day if you have to . . . but still call, text, or e-mail someone sometimes.

Save some things for later.

Personally, I love dark, quirky entertainment—*Sherlock, Mad Men, Doctor Who* episodes like "Blink," almost anything Tim Burton—but know now to set it aside during depressive cycles. It's all too easy to identify with the clearly troubled Draper kids or (worst case) Sweeney Todd; also, too much death is unhealthy.

Whatever your favorite poison, don't take it while you're depressed. *Twilight Zone* reruns will always be there. They'll never stop making vampire movies. You don't have to watch Baby Shark videos, for love of God; just lighten up a little for a while.

Save some people for later.

The one exception to the "Don't isolate" tip is people who make you crazy *and* whom you can avoid. Pop psychologists love to yammer nonsense about "toxic people," but you know what they mean, so try steering clear of people who make you feel tainted: squirrelly acquaintances, snoopy neighbors, interfering relatives, all frenemies without exception. And always, *always* keep at least a pitchfork's distance from anyone who says things like these:

- "It's all in your head." (Duh.)
- "You're too sensitive."
- "You're not the only one who has troubles."
- "What do *you* have to be depressed about?"
- "Do you know what your problem is?"
  (That last one is the absolute worst.)

When you're feeling better, if you want to or have to deal with these types, that's your business. Just try to give them a miss till then.

Remember that cycles repeat.

You were up; now you're down; soon you'll be up again. Manic depression is like weather, sort of. No matter how dark and stormy the night, keep reminding yourself that it won't last and that you've lived through weather before.

If you don't like that simile, try thinking of your depressive cycle as a turn of a wheel—perhaps roulette. The Persephone–Hades myth is a good one too.

Eat ice cream.

Mint chocolate chip is particularly medicinal.
Feel better.

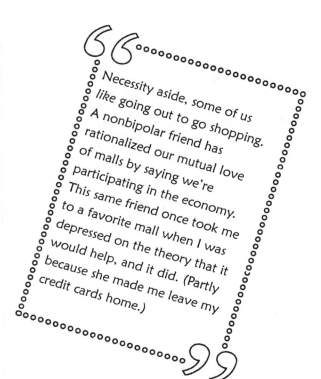

" Necessity aside, some of us like going out to go shopping. A nonbipolar friend has rationalized our mutual love of malls by saying we're participating in the economy. This same friend once took me to a favorite mall when I was depressed on the theory that it would help, and it did. (Partly because she made me leave my credit cards home.) "

Clker-Free-Vector-Images / Pixabay

geralt / Pixabay

There's one more depression-buster we haven't discussed—a natural, drug-free, short-term fix you wouldn't expect.

Staying up all night.

Sounds crazy, right? But it works. A 2011 article in *Psychology Today* cited more than 60 studies that confirm it.

Researchers have been looking at this effect since the 1970s and still don't quite know *why* it works. But a team of neuroscientists at University of California-Berkeley has found that limited deprivation of REM sleep activates the brain's reward networks, most likely by increasing dopamine levels.

Dopamine would do it. Wellbutrin (bupropion), for example, is a dopamine reuptake inhibitor, which is to say an antidepressant that keeps this mood-boosting brain chemical flowing. Which is why a whole class of antidepressants specifically targets dopamine and norepinephrine. Chapter 9 breaks all this down in excruciating detail.

In other words, whatever elevates low dopamine levels can lift depression, and one of those whatevers is sleep deprivation. I found this out by accident one night in my early 20s when I was too depressed to sleep and didn't. (Coffee and a large record collection helped.) By dawn, the depression was gone. I went to work as usual that day and felt *terrific*. But then I slept. As researchers have noted, the effect is temporary.

Sleep deprivation has serious physical and mental effects over time, of course, so don't do it more than one night in a row. Also, this trick may work best when you're young and more or less bulletproof.

But if you're way, way down and the meds aren't working (or haven't kicked in yet), you might give staying up all night a try. Think how much Netflix you could catch up on!

Catering
to
Depressives

The day when Amazon delivers everything isn't far distant. One of my sisters-in-law has Alexa order household staples for her on a regular basis, and if paper towels can spontaneously appear on customers' doorsteps, I suppose we're already at the thin edge of the wedge.

Still, delivery of everything is a fantastic idea for depressed (*and financially responsible!*) manic-depressives, especially now that groceries can come to your very door. If you don't have children, pets, partners, plants, or business to tend to, you could easily wait out your depressive cycle on the couch, getting up only to fetch cartons of food from the porch every so often.

Hey, do you think Amazon could deliver ice cream in a bowl with the spoon already in it?

Eugenio Hansen, OFS / Pixabay

The devil has put a penalty on all things we enjoy in life. Either we suffer in health or we suffer in soul or we get fat.

— *Albert Einstein*

Did you see the movie? If so, you'll know about Alex, the offscreen character who killed himself. Your guess is as good as mine, but my guess is that the fictional Alex had the real bipolar disorder. Bipolars have a *very* high risk of suicide.

These days, people in general are at high risk. Consider:

The Bipolar Big Chill

- Suicide is the 10th-leading cause of death in the United States, the #2 cause of death among people ages 10 to 34, and the #4 cause of death among those 35 to 54.
- From 1999 to 2016, suicides increased by 20 percent in more than half the states.
- There were more than 47,000 suicides and 1.4 million attempts in the United States in 2017 alone.
- Fully 90 percent of people who commit suicide had a mental illness at time of death.

These are grim numbers. They're grimmer still for BP IIs. We spend more time than other bipolars in depression, which differs from both the shorter BP I cycle and unipolar depression. BP IIs are down longer, deeper, and darker, with what NIMH calls "a substantially more chronic course, with significantly more major and minor depressive episodes and shorter inter-episode well intervals."

That's bad. Here's worse: An estimated 32.4 percent of people with bipolar II disorder will attempt suicide over their lifetimes. Compare that figure with the 4.3 percent of the general adult population who think about it (lifetime ideation) but don't necessarily act.

If you have BP II, your life may literally depend on knowing when you need help.

If you're in crisis, go to your local emergency room, dial 911, call a local hotline, or call this one:

National Suicide Prevention Lifeline, 800-273-TALK (8255)
Webchat at https://suicidepreventionlifeline.org/chat

Finally, remember that **suicide is a permanent solution to a temporary problem**.

By the time you read this chapter, a three-digit national suicide hotline number could be in business.

The National Suicide Hotline Improvement Act of 2018 replaced 800-273-TALK with 988, which sponsors said would be easier to remember and faster to dial in a crisis. For reasons that are unclear, the chairman of the Federal Communications Commission (FCC) at the time claimed that the new number will also minimize stigma.

Guess we'll find out in July 2022--the target launch date for 988.

As of press time, I couldn't find any single resource to check for updates, so your best bet is to check with your carrier—and keep 911 in the back of your head in the meantime.

Chapter 8

Both (and More)

Both

Mixed states are the Jekyll and Hyde of bipolar disorder (except that you can see them together). They're also like Superman and Clark Kent (except that Lois Lane couldn't possibly have been dumb enough *not* to figure that out).

You might even say that they're like Sybil, Eve, or any other multiple-personality types (except that multiple personality is called disassociative identity disorder now and is a whole different kettle of fish from bipolar).

> Bipolars who experience mixed states may require *combination therapy*—treatment with multiple drugs. Atypical antipsychotics seem to be most effective. (National Center for Biotechnology Information [NCBI])

Short definition from MedicineNet: A *mixed state* in bipolar disorder is "the occurrence of symptoms of mania and depression together. A person may feel sad and hopeless while at the same time feeling extremely energized. Also called *dysphoric mania, mixed mania,* or *agitated depression*."

Well, *that's* not good, is it?

I've never experienced a certified mixed state. But I've had flashes of agitation during depression and transient blue moods during hypomania, which may be what a mixed state feels like.

Mostly: confusing.

My experience is of strange interruptions—flashes of contradictory emotions that come without warning and go the same way. For want of a better word, let's call them *mixes*. Mixes aren't the cycles that define manic depression; they're fleeting waves of feeling. Neither are they that soppy "laughing through tears" thing or ordinary mixed emotions. They're slightly alien and remote—a bit like Harry Potter sensing Lord Voldemort's moods. (Voldemort isn't a bad analogy.)

For me, a mix is a flare of anger or irritation for no reason while I'm feeling good. The anger is much too short-lived to be a mood cycle or even a mood. I don't know what it is. But it's as close as I've been to a mixed state. (Probably.)

Experts say that mixed states are common, with roughly half of bipolars experiencing them at one time or another. Often, the mania/hypomania and depression are *subsyndromal* (not severe enough to warrant bipolar diagnosis), which is one reason why many bipolars aren't properly diagnosed for years. But *DSM-5* (Chapter 4) suggests the specifier *mixed features*, which includes subsyndromal symptoms. See "Mixed Up (and Down)" in this chapter for details on mixed features in mania/hypomania and depression.

> Everything flows and nothing abides, everything gives way and nothing stays fixed.
> — Heraclitus

> Better not bring up a lion inside your city, But if you must, then humor all his moods.
> — Aristophanes, *Frogs*

More

This book majors in BP II, with a minor in BP I and a concentration in comorbidities. Academically, however, bipolar disorder falls into four major classes (Chapter 4):

- Bipolar I
- Bipolar II
- Cyclothymia
- Bipolar Disorder Not Otherwise Specified

These categories aren't absolute. Some antidepressants and stimulants can trigger manic episodes in people who have any flavor of bipolar, even in those who don't have BP I. Also, there's overlap. Worse, patients who have BP II could transition to BP I; some researchers believe that BP II is BP I in potentia.

Really not good. Worth being aware of, though.

To qualify as having a manic/hypomanic episode with mixed features, a bipolar must exhibit three of the following symptoms for most of that cycle:

- Depressed mood
- Feelings of worthlessness or guilt
- Loss of interest in or enjoyment of pleasurable activities
- Slower-than-usual movement, with fatigue
- Suicidal thoughts

For a depressive episode with mixed features, three of the following symptoms must be present during most of the cycle:

- Significantly elevated mood
- Grandiose behavior
- Increased energy
- Unusual talkativeness
- Racing thoughts
- Reckless activity
- Short sleep

Mixed Up (and Down)

Gordon Johnson / Pixabay

Tour de Bipolar: Rapid Cycling

sabinevanerp / Pixabay

Then there's rapid cycling. This pattern is fairly rare in bipolar disorder, affecting perhaps 10 to 20 percent of those who have it, but BP IIs of all genders and all bipolar women are most likely to experience it.

Rapid cycling is defined by frequent, distinct mood swings, with four or more manic/hypomanic and depressive cycles in a year. Most rapid cyclers spend longer in depression than in mania/hypomania or mixed states, but that's the general rule for BP IIs anyway.

Not everyone who rapid-cycles does so like clockwork; the pattern can appear and disappear randomly, making it hard to identify. Further, rapid cycling isn't always a switch between distinct states. A person who has this pattern may have fluctuations in a single episode of mania/hypomania or depression, but because the episode itself doesn't resolve, the rapid cycling may go unnoticed.

Most doctors prescribe mood stabilizers as first-line treatment for rapid cycling. Even though the pattern leans more to depression than to mania or hypomania, antidepressants seem to be ineffective and may even speed the cycles, but they might be used short-term when the depression is severe. See Chapter 9 for details on these medications and others.

French journalist/cyclist Henri Desgrange started the Tour de France in 1903 as a circulation-boosting promotion for his paper *L'Auto*. The yellow jersey (*maillot jaune*) worn by the overall general-classification leader after each stage—the rapidest cycler, if you like—is yellow because *L'Auto* was printed on yellow paper. (Britannica.com)

Part 4

Getting Better

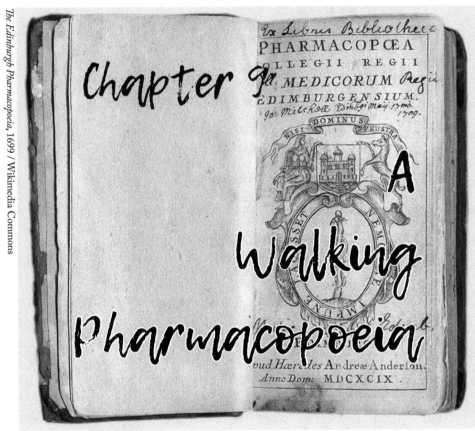

Chapter 9a

A Walking Pharmacopoeia

For a few years there, if you'd had occasion to shake me, I'd have rattled. Doctors prescribed pill after pill after pill in those days, mostly for unipolar depression. Being a good patient (then), I took whatever was prescribed exactly as prescribed, asking no questions and lodging no complaints.

Boy, has *that* changed.

Before I tell you why, let me tell you a little about what it was like to be a human pillbox.

These are a few psychoactive medications I remember having taken . . . and not. Some were self-prescribed. (For details on these and other meds, see "The Well-Equipped Bipolar's Apothecary" in this chapter.)

Antidepressants: taken
Asendin (amoxapine; tricyclic)
Elavil (amitryptiline; tricyclic)
Norpramin (desipramine; tricyclic)
Pamelor (nortryptiline; tricyclic)
Paxil (paroxetine; SSRI)
Prozac (fluoxetine; SSRI)
Remeron (mirtazapine; atypical)
Serzone (nefazodone; atypical)
Tofranil (imipramine; tricyclic)
Wellbutrin (bupropion; atypical)*
Zoloft (sertraline; SSRI)

Antidepressants: prescribed but not taken
Celexa (citalopram)
Desyrel (trazodone)
Effexor (venlafaxine)
Lexapro (escitalopram)

Anxiolytics (antianxiety)
BuSpar (buspirone)
Valium (diazepam)
Xanax (alprazolam)

Mood stabilizers
Lamictal (lamotrigine; antiepileptic)
Neurontin (gabapentin; anticonvulsant)

Sedatives
Restoril (temaxepam)
Also: Anxiolytics
Also: Other

Stimulants
Adderall XR (amphetamine/dextroamphetamine mixed salts)
Coffee, black tea, more coffee (caffeine)
Marlboro Red (nicotine; cigarettes)
Nicoderm/Nicoderm CQ (nicotine; patch)
Nicorette (nicotine; gum)
Salem Light 100s (nicotine; cigarettes)
Sudafed (pseudoephedrine; decongestant; sometimes used off-label)**
True Green (nicotine; cigarettes)
Whatever other cigarettes were on hand (nicotine)

Other
Alcohol, especially the sauvignons (Cabernet and blanc)
LSD (once)
Marijuana

As you see, I like stimulants. Also, I certainly took more antidepressants than are listed here, but they were prescribed so long ago that I've forgotten their names—and/or the hospital nurses didn't say what was in all those little paper pill cups.

As for the downers, alcohol has always been only a sometime thing, and the only trouble I ever had with pot was forgetting to order pizza ahead of the munchies.

---

* Also prescribed as Zyban for smoking cessation. But I smoked—a lot —the whole time I took Wellbutrin, so you may want to be skeptical.

** *Not* for meth.

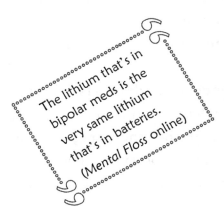

The lithium that's in bipolar meds is the very same lithium that's in batteries. (Mental Floss online)

Whenever psychoactive drugs come to mind, I like to think of Jefferson Airplane's "White Rabbit." No pill of this type can make the taker larger or small; still, it amuses me to believe that Wonderland is in a capsule. (Secretly, I think, all bipolars hope so.)

But even though the "White Rabbit" effect is fiction, real psychiatric meds have real side effects, some of which are worrisome. The FDA and NIMH break down the most common of them this way:

Antidepressants
Nausea and vomiting
Weight gain
Diarrhea
Drowsiness
Sexual problems

Anxiolytics and sedatives
Nausea
Blurred vision
Headache
Confusion

Fatigue
Nightmares

Mood stabilizers
Itching and/or rash
Excessive thirst
Frequent urination
Tremor
Nausea and vomiting
Slurred speech
Fast, slow, irregular, or pounding heartbeat

Blackouts
Changes in vision
Seizures
Hallucinations
Loss of coordination
Swelling

Stimulants
Trouble sleeping
Loss of appetite
Stomach pain
Headache

While we're at it, another class of psychoactive drugs may be used to treat bipolar disorder (more in BP I than in BP II):

Antipsychotics
Drowsiness
Dizziness
Restlessness
Weight gain
Dry mouth
Constipation

Nausea and vomiting
Blurred vision
Low blood pressure
Tics and tremors
Seizures
Decrease in white blood cells

Alarming, no? Once upon a time, I never bothered reading the patient information that comes with prescription drugs; now I do, and it usually gives me the willies. That's one reason why I stopped taking psychoactive drugs for 20-odd years. Most of those meds were expensive and didn't even work except for side effects, so what was the point?

I know better now than to self-diagnose (Chapter 4). Medications *do* have side effects, but you won't necessarily get all of them, or any, and the benefits may outweigh the potential risks.

Still, I'm unusually medication-sensitive and have to be more cautious than the average bipolar. If you have trouble with side effects too, don't suffer in silence: Tell your doctor. Time, slower titration, or a change of dose may solve the problem. If not, another med may work better *and* be easier on you.

Still no good? Consider getting genetically tested to find out exactly what you can take safely (see "Your Skin-Tight Genes" in this chapter).

As for reading the fine print in patient information, I can't say not to. In fact, you probably should: Information is power. But you probably shouldn't be too rattled by it. Most of the warnings are about rare reactions, included mostly as a legal CYA move. Pharmaceuticals go through years of testing before FDA approval, with hundreds of healthy test subjects taking them in clinical trials, and if any subject's brain had exploded, the drug would've (well, *should've*) gone back to the pharma company's drawing board.

Know the warning signs of adverse effects; ask your doctor if you have concerns; then try to sleep well at night. Your brain isn't likely to explode after one or two doses of any medication.

(If it does, though, the FDA will want to know.)

For the lowdown on the whole pharmacopoeia, see "The Well-Equipped Bipolar's Apothecary" in this chapter.

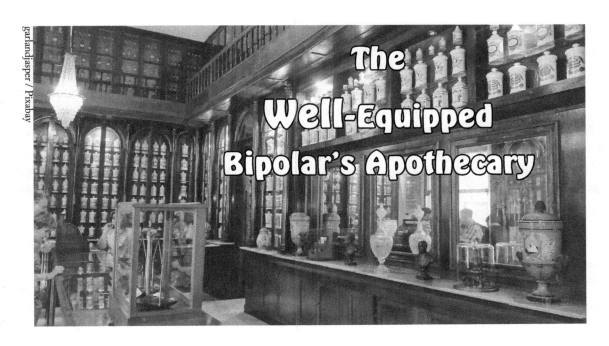

garlandjasper / Pixabay

Following are some of the drugs that are used to treat bipolar disorder. Your personal stash may vary.

Anti-
d
e
p
r
e
s
s
a
n
t
s

Atypicals
    Examples: Wellbutrin (bupropion) and Remeron (mirtazapine)
MAOIs (monoamine oxidase inhibitors)
    Examples: Nardil (phenelzine) and Parnate (tranylcypromine)
SARIs (serotonin antagonist and reuptake inhibitors)
    Examples: Serzone (nefazodone) and Desyrel (trazodone)
SNRIs (serotonin-norepinephrine reuptake inhibitors)
    Examples: Cymbalta (duloxetine) and Pristiq (desvenlafaxine)
SSRIs (selective serotonin reuptake inhibitors)
    Examples: Prozac (fluoxetine) and Celexa (citalopram)
Tetracyclics
    Examples: Ascendin (amoxapine) and Ludiomil (maprotiline)
Tricyclics
    Examples: Elavil (amitryptiline) and Norpramin (desipramine)

These medications travel in packs.

A few antidepressants fall into multiple categories, for reasons that it would take a pharmacist to explain. Ask one if you're curious.

For laypersons' purposes, the most important thing to know is that antidepressants have different courses of action, targeting different neurotransmitters, sometimes blocking the *reuptake* (reabsorption) of specific neurotransmitters into the brain's nerve cells. Most people are familiar with SSRIs, the best-known of which arguably is Prozac. MAOIs and tricyclics may be less familiar, being older and seldom prescribed now due to side effects (both) and dietary restrictions (MAOIs).

Warning: Never stop taking an antidepressant cold and without your doctor's knowledge. Withdrawal from some drugs without tapering can be brutal. For a cautionary tale, see "Christmas in Hell: Serotonin Syndrome" in this chapter.

Antidepressants and sedatives are often prescribed for anxiety, but so are *anxiolytics*: medications specifically developed to inhibit anxiety. Like antidepressants, some of these drugs have multiple effects. They fall into these categories:

A
n
x
i
o
l
y
t
i
c
s

Barbiturates
　　Examples: Seconal (secobarbital) and Nembutal (pentobarbital)
Benzodiazepines
　　Examples: Valium (diazepam) and Xanax (alprazolam)
Other sedatives and hypnotics
　　Examples: Ambien (zolpidem) and Lunesta (eszopiclone)

Barbiturates, which were widely used from the 1950s through the 1970s, are rarely prescribed today; benzodiazepines* have fewer side effects and are considered to be safer.

Incidentally, you may have sung along with a Rolling Stones song about an anxiolytic: "Mother's Little Helper," which hit No. 8 in 1966. Some people claim that "Helper" is about Valium, but Gizmodo says it's about Miltown (meprobamate). Let's go with Gizmodo, because Miltown was a notorious favorite of women in the '50s and '60s. You don't hear much about it anymore, possibly thanks in part to the Stones.

Mood stabilizers

Don't be confused by the fact that some of these drugs are anticonvulsants and antiepileptics. They aren't just for treating epilepsy; they're also used to stabilize moods in bipolar disorder. Examples include Tegretol (carbamazepine), Neurontin (gabapentin), and Lamictal (lamotrigine), all of which have proved to be particularly effective against bipolar depression. Tegretol, Lamictal, and Depakote (valproate) appear to work well for acute mania, mixed states, and rapid cycling (Chapter 8). One study found that lithium (see "Light Metal: Lithium" in this chapter) is more effective for all these conditions, but many manic-depressives can't tolerate lithium due to its side effects and frequent required lab tests, making anticonvulsants or antiepileptics better options for them.

Sedatives

In other words, sleeping pills, and you know about those. Many of these same meds—Valium, Xanax, Ambien, and the like—are also used as anxiolytics. If you haven't taken them yourself, you know people who have.

The same goes for alcohol, which is another widely used sedative.

Stimulants

As noted earlier, I love them. I've used stimulants since college and will keep using them to the end (and probably beyond).

My personal drugs of choice are caffeine, nicotine, and Adderall. I quit smoking for good in 2003, so nicotine is out now. But as long as there are Starbucks locations, local coffeehouses, and coffee beans by the bag, caffeine will be my first-line stimulant.

For ADHD, I take Adderall XR (amphetamine/dextroamphetamine mixed salts) as needed. It works so well that I'm tempted to take it every day, but I take it under medical supervision, which disapproves of long-term daily use. Other popular prescription stimulants are Ritalin (methylphenidate), Focalin (dexmethylphenidate), and Vyvanse (lisdexamfetamine).

Other

This category is a catch-all, encompassing everything from recreational and other prescription drugs to sketchy OTC pills and potions to nice frosty (and salt-rimmed) margaritas. If it affects your mind, it's psychoactive.

Those of us who take bipolar meds should use substances in this category sparingly, if at all, and with caution. The more meds of any kind you take (including birth-control pills; see Chapter 11), the more abstemious and careful you should be. Before starting a new medication, ask your doctor and/or pharmacist about potential interactions with alcohol and other substances.

It goes without saying (but I'm saying it anyway) that if you have bipolar disorder *and* a history of substance abuse, it's risky to go anywhere near any of these things.

---

* Benzodiazepines are not to be confused with *bennies*, which is slang for Benzedrine (amphetamine sulfate).

For all I've said here about the boatloads of psychoactive drugs I've taken, it's not easy to get boatloads these days. Many hospitals and medical practices have started restricting certain medications, including psychoactives.

Take stimulants. Dr. H. prescribed Adderall XR years ago with no fuss whatsoever, but when I asked Dr. J. for a new scrip, he read me chapter and verse of the practice's new policy. To get the med, he said, I'd have to go to counseling first. Then, *if* he prescribed it, I'd have to keep coming back for lab tests. Even though he had a detailed report from the psychologist who diagnosed severe ADHD, even though I'd taken the drug safely before, even though genetic testing would soon clear me to take *all* stimulants (see "Your Skin-Tight Genes" in this chapter), counseling and labs were non-negotiable.

Nuts. After multiple hospitalizations and years of talk therapy, I wasn't going through counseling again for a few caps of ADHD meds. Neither was I on board with having all those labs.

Dr. M. wrote the prescription in the end. He's a psychiatrist, and Dr. J. is an internist, which I suppose made the difference. But *still*.

T., on the other hand, jumped through those hoops for lithium. He'd been formally diagnosed with bipolar disorder but still had to have four sessions of counseling before getting the medication. He also had to have regular labs for a while. (But those checks are absolutely, positively necessary for people who are new to this drug; see "Light Metal: Lithium" in this chapter.)

I have no anecdotal evidence of strict prescribing requirements for popular antidepressants. And many anxiolytics (such as Xanax and Valium) fall under Schedule IV of the U.S. Controlled Substances Act, which the U.S. Drug Enforcement Administration (DEA) describes as "drugs with a low potential for abuse and low risk of dependence."* So you're probably safe enough asking your family doctor, internist, or nurse practitioner for SSRIs or sleeping pills. For anything riskier or more exotic, be prepared for counseling/testing requirements.

By the way, it turns out that regular Adderall and the XR version are Schedule II drugs. The DEA describes them thusly: "Schedule II drugs, substances, or chemicals are defined as drugs with a high potential for abuse, with use potentially leading to severe psychological or physical dependence. These drugs are also considered dangerous."

All right, then. Dr. J.'s practice was playing safe over sorry, and he was following protocol. Doesn't mean I have to like it.

* I saw the effects of Xanax addiction in a psychiatric hospital and beg to differ, but I'm only a manic-depressive; what do I know?

Pay for Your Meds

No matter what Big Pharma ads or pharma-company detailers might tell you, patented psychiatric meds are beyond expensive, and latest isn't always greatest. One new drug that's supposed to work for bipolar depression, for example, is *beyond* beyond expensive: In my area of the country, a 30-day supply costs more than $1,300. (Not a typo.) And if you think you'll just wait for the generic, you'll be waiting 12 years . . . or longer.

Sure, your doctor might give you samples. But how many? And for how long? And will your insurance pay when you finally have to pick up the tab yourself?

Get mad. Then get busy:

- If you have insurance, check your policy's *formulary* (list of covered medications), and make sure that you know what your co-pay for a med would be—both before and after you meet your deductible.
- Should the news be bad, or if you don't have insurance, ask your doctor to prescribe an older med that's available in generic form.
- If you can't get a generic, ask your pharmacy whether a GoodRx coupon for a name-brand drug would be cheaper than your insurance co-pay. (Keep in mind that if you go that route, the cost won't apply to your deductible.)
- Ask the manufacturer, the government, and/or not-for-profit agencies for help paying for your meds. You'll find a detailed list of these resources at https://www.nami.org/Find-Support/Living-with-a-Mental-Health-Condition/Getting-Help-Paying-for-Medications.

Mary Poppins was smoking crack with that spoonful-of-sugar business, if you ask me. I took her advice once as a child and never again, because swallowing something smooth with something gritty is disconcerting and weird. Plain water helps the medicine go down fine.

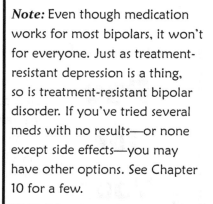

Note: Even though medication works for most bipolars, it won't for everyone. Just as treatment-resistant depression is a thing, so is treatment-resistant bipolar disorder. If you've tried several meds with no results—or none except side effects—you may have other options. See Chapter 10 for a few.

Take Your Meds

But if sugar helps you, great. Use it. Do whatever works. Just take your meds. Reports say that more than 75 percent of patients take them less than 75 percent of the time, and I know two things from experience: (1) Medicine won't work if you don't take it, and (2) Your doctor will look at you like this if you don't.

Gellinger / Pixabay

In addition to taking them period, take them on time. This can be harder than it sounds. Some of us are absent-minded and forget when it's time for a pill; others of us are passive-aggressive and forget on purpose. Whatever your mindset, if you've had trouble staying on track with your medications, try using a reminder app or setting a repeating alarm on your smartphone. Come up with *some* ritual that works.

And if you forget whether you've taken what you should (it happens), it may help to make a list of your daily meds and check off each dose after you take it. Scratch paper is fine for this purpose. A chalkboard or whiteboard will work too as long as you have exclusive rights to it. (Never assume that housemates and/or loved ones would resist embellishing your work.)

If all else fails, turn each vial upside down on its cap after you've taken your pill(s). Just remember to turn it right-side up again ahead of the next dose.

Routine matters in this matter, for two reasons:

• The more often you do something, the more muscle memory you build, and muscle memory can take over when the other kind fails. (Being absent-minded, I sometimes find myself walking into the kitchen around meds time and forgetting why but automatically opening the meds cabinet.)

• It takes two weeks to develop a habit. After that, your medication-taking routine should feel familiar. Or at least less *un*familiar, which amounts to the same thing.

Light Metal: Lithium

You've heard of it, surely, and may be lithium-curious. Lithium has been around for ages (it was first used in psychiatry during the 19th century) and is one of the most-studied psychoactive meds on the market. It's straight from nature—a soft alkaline metal and chemical element often found in mineral springs—and like many things in nature (see Chapter 10), lithium has the power to stabilize moods. Perhaps its best-known use is in acute mania, which occurs in BP I, but studies have found it to be useful in bipolar depression, so some doctors prescribe it for BP IIs.

Lithium (technically, lithium carbonate) is a generic that's also prescribed under the brand names Eskalith and Lithobid. It comes in a variety of forms, including tablets, capsules, and liquids. Whatever it's named and however it comes, it's a miracle drug for many manic-depressives.

Now the bad news. Lithium can also be harmful—so harmful that the FDA issued a black-box warning for it. This type of warning, which appears on labels and in patient information, calls attention to serious, possibly life-threatening dangers. Reason: Even at or near therapeutic levels, lithium can be toxic. As a result, new users generally have to get frequent lab tests, drink lots of water, and consume very little salt (to keep serum levels of the medication from spiking). What's more, lithium has a long, daunting list of side effects* for about three-quarters of users.

> "Lithium has been found to reduce the thinning of gray matter in the brains of manic-depressives. It also alters brain signatures; the same is true of antiepileptic and antipsychotic medications. (University of Southern California)"

Just as Coca-Cola once got its kick from cocaine (1886 to 1929), 7UP contained lithium citrate from 1929 to 1950. You may recall the 7UP slogan "You Like It. It Likes You." What with lithium in it, no wonder.

Should you be leery of lithium? Depends. The definition of acceptable risk is up to you and your doctor. Newer mood stabilizers tend to have lower side-effect profiles, which may make them better choices if you're medication-sensitive. But it's only fair to point out that many antidepressants also have black-box warnings (paradoxically, for increased suicide risk); so do a couple of medications commonly prescribed for mania and/or bipolar depression. Whether or not you ever take lithium, as a manic-depressive, you're likely to take *some* black-box-warned drug at some point.

Don't panic overmuch, though. As my internist keeps saying, every drug has side effects. Lithium may cause more than most medications, but it wouldn't have been on the market this long if it weren't safe and effective for many bipolars. Follow your doctor's directions exactly to minimize the risks and maximize the benefits.

* I counted 81 "less common," "rare," and "incidence not known" side effects for lithium on Drugs.com in March 2020.

VintageBlue / Pixabay

The hat didn't help.

Of the many psychiatric compounds I've taken, the one I'll never, *ever* take again is Paxil. Yes, it works for millions of people every day with perfect safety and efficacy, and I have nothing bad whatsoever to say about the drug itself. The problem is how it was prescribed in my case: carelessly.

The psychiatrist in question was a posthospitalization referral. We didn't click, exactly, but he came highly recommended, so it was logical to assume that he knew his business. We'd tried several SSRIs that fall with little result except side effects. (This is normal for misdiagnosed manic-depressives; see Chapter 4.) I can't remember everything he prescribed because he changed meds at almost every appointment.

Finally, the day before the Christmas holidays, this doctor—let's call him Quack (I forget his real name)—decided that the current med was no good either and that it was time for yet another SSRI.

Dr. Q. wrote a prescription for Paxil. Then he sent me off for Christmas with the airy assurance that it was fine to stop my current antidepressant and start the new one the next morning.

I did. Soon after, I was sick. But when I called Dr. Q.'s office, no one was in. A recording said that the doctor was out of town, unreachable until the first week of January . . . and by the way, there was no emergency number.

Not knowing what else to do, and still being depressed, I kept taking Paxil for a few more days. Finally, I quit it cold—which is the worst thing to do with this med. Most of what followed is a blur now. But I clearly remember fever, chills, inability to be vertical, and a vicious sick headache that lasted days.

What I had was *serotonin syndrome*—high levels of the brain chemical serotonin in the body, which can make a person dangerously ill. Some antidepressants, pain medications, OTC supplements, and cough/cold medicines are linked to serotonin syndrome; they're listed a few paragraphs down. The SSRIs include Paxil. They surely include the other antidepressant that was still in my system—and should *not* have been—when I started the Paxil. Almost certainly, I was also taking OTC cold medicine.

Thanks to genetic testing last summer, I now know that this experience was a quadruple whammy. Besides having three serotonin-syndrome-associated meds in my bloodstream at the time, I had—*have*—a gene that makes it impossible to take Paxil safely. (For more on genetic testing, see "Your Skin-Tight Genes" in this chapter.)

Obviously, I survived. Eventually, the worst was over, and if it wasn't all sunshine and bluebirds at my house, it wasn't Mozart's *Requiem** either. I don't remember what I said to Dr. Q. when he got back to the office, but the phone line would have been smoking for weeks.

If memory serves, I didn't take psychiatric meds again for the next 20 years.

Serotonin syndrome develops quickly—often within hours of starting a drug or increasing the dose. It's always unpleasant, but with luck, it's mild. In severe cases and without proper treatment, it can be fatal.

For this reason alone, you should know the symptoms:

- Agitation
- Confusion
- Fast heartbeat
- High blood pressure
- Dilated pupils

- Loss of coordination and/or muscle twitches
- Sweating
- Diarrhea
- Headache
- Chills

These additional symptoms may be present in severe cases:

- High fever
- Seizures
- Uneven heartbeat
- Fainting

In mild cases, stopping the drug should solve the problem in a day or two. But *always* seek medical treatment or at least advice. If you're very ill and can't reach the prescribing doctor, get yourself to the nearest emergency room.

You can lessen your chance of developing serotonin syndrome by being up front with your doctor about everything you take, and how much of it. The following medications are often associated with the syndrome. This list is Mayo Clinic's (and for brevity, I'll use brand names where possible):

- Antidepressants, including
    - SSRIs
    - SNRIs
    - Atypicals
    - Tricyclics
    - MAOIs
- Opioids, including
    - Fentanyl
    - OxyContin
    - Demerol
    - Tylenol with codeine
- Prescription migraine medications, including
    - Imitrex
    - Tegretol
    - Depakene

- Prescription nausea medications, including
    - Reglan
    - Inapsine
    - Zofran
- The antibiotic Zyvox and the anti-retroviral Norvir
- OTC herbal supplements, including
    - St. John's wort
    - Ginseng
    - Nutmeg
- OTC cough/cold medicines that contain dextromethorphan, including
    - Delsym
    - Mucinex DM
- Recreational drugs

Your doctor or pharmacy should do interaction checks as a matter of course, but as mentioned in Chapter 5, these checks are only as good as your medical history. Make sure that it's complete, including OTC and recreational drugs. (You shouldn't be doing the second kind while taking psychiatric medication.)

And by the way, never let a doctor start you on a new med right before a holiday—not even you have his or her number *and* a promise to pick up if called. Otherwise, you may be under the wing of a Quack.

---

* Formally: Requiem in D minor, K. 626.

Your Skin-Tight Genes

Never mind the line in the Katy Perry hit.* Here, of course, we're talking *genes*. Specifically, we're talking *pharmacogenomics testing—genetic drug testing* for purposes of this discussion.

Long story short, this type of test determines your levels of certain enzymes—enzymes that affect your body's ability to break down (*metabolize*) certain medications. If you can't metabolize a drug efficiently, you may have high or low serum concentrations, which can make you more susceptible to side effects.

Genes aren't the only determinants of drug metabolism, however. Harvard Medical School says that age, gender, dietary and smoking habits, medical history, and other medications affect it too. The balance between genetics and these other factors varies widely, in that genes may be responsible for a sliver of metabolism or for nearly the whole pie. For this reason, genetic testing won't necessarily return definitive answers.

So is it worthwhile?

Depends who you ask. Plenty of people swear by these tests; some have horror stories to tell. Doctors and insurance companies don't always agree on the validity of the results or the utility of the testing. There are concerns about the industry's lack of FDA regulation. And although genetic drug testing is becoming more accessible and affordable, without insurance, it can cost more than $5,000.

In other words, read the fine print in your insurance policy; then have a serious talk with your doctor about whether genetic drug testing is right for you.

It was right for me. As noted again and again, I've taken many psychiatric drugs, the most troublesome of which were SSRI antidepressants, which did little if any therapeutic good and caused awful side effects. I complained to all the doctors who insisted on prescribing SSRIs, but their advice was always to wait a few months, or take aspirin, or take a flying leap.

These doctors' insistence on prescribing drugs I couldn't tolerate was due in part to misdiagnosis of my bipolar disorder as plain-vanilla major depression. (Antidepressants rarely help bipolars and frequently make them worse.) Also, these meds were so popular that the ads told patients to ask for them, and some pharma-company detailers pressured—or paid—doctors to prescribe them. On extra-cynical days, I suspect that some of my doctors were corrupt, narcissistic jerks who Knew It All despite unimpeachable evidence to the contrary.

The SSRI situation is another reason why I stopped taking psychiatric meds for years.

So when Dr. J. suggested going back on antidepressants, I said no. When he suggested genetic testing, however, I said yes. Any chance of reducing trial-and-error—and side effects—is a chance I'll take.

The test itself was a painless cheek swab, and the results came back in less than two weeks.

Guess what? I don't metabolize most SSRIs well, which means that they get highly concentrated in my bloodstream and are very likely to cause side effects. Guess what else? The SSRI that caused serotonin syndrome (see "Christmas in Hell" in this chapter) is so dangerous for me that the test said not to take it. Never ever.

(Note to doctors: *Told you.*)

The two medications I take these days have long, alarming lists of side effects, but (so far) they've been safe and effective for me—as my genes said they would be.

Getting tested is a personal, medical, and possibly financial decision, although some companies charge on a sliding scale based on income. According to Harvard Med, you may benefit from genetic drug testing if you have a history of severe side effects and/or failed medication response.

That's me to a T; maybe it's you too.

* "Teenage Dream," from the 2010 Capitol album of the same name.

Where Do These Screwy Drug Names Come From?

All of us have seen too many commercials for pharmaceuticals. The medications differ, but the pitches are always the same. I don't know about you, but I mute the sound *and* leave the room when they come on.

> Consultants aren't responsible for all the preposterous drug names in the world. Pharma companies have come up with generic names such as idebenone (Alzheimer's disease), pancuronium bromide (muscle relaxant), and xylometazoline (decongestant). (*The Week* online)

Among the worst features of these ads are the drug names, which range from dumb to downright Martian. It's not unreasonable to assume that the pharma companies put random words in a hopper and let the CEO's dog pull a few out. That assumption would be wrong, though. Did you know that there are things called "name engineering agencies" and "pharmaceutical naming consultancies"?

The process that leads to screwball drug names begins when a pharmaceutical company's chemists create a new molecule. This molecule goes through many phases of refinement and testing under a generic name that's based on chemical makeup. At some point along the way, the drug also acquires a brand name, often devised by one of the aforementioned concerns. When the drug is finally submitted to the FDA for approval, two departments in that agency review the proposed brand name. And according to CNN, up to 35 percent of those names are rejected.

In a world with phensuximide and Luzu, you have to wonder what drug name could be bad enough to *be* rejected.

Chapter 10

Shrunk: Beyond Meds

So much for pharmaceutical treatment (Chapter 9). Now let's talk about psychotherapy, a/k/a talk therapy.

Nearly all bipolars will be offered psychotherapy at some point, normally after they're pretty well stabilized chemically. It's hard to talk to *anyone* during active hypomania or depression, let alone to a stranger who writes down everything you say and keeps asking, "How do you feel about that?" There are exceptions, such as emergency interventions, but most manic-depressives start with medication and then move on to talk.

Do you *have* to move on to it? Not necessarily. Even good health insurance may cover only 30 mental-health therapy visits a year, so you may be reluctant to start what you can't afford to finish. But your therapist will probably recommend going for the 30, and not just to run up a tab. Studies have shown that bipolars who get both medication and psychotherapy do better than those who get monotherapy. Moreover, psychotherapy generally works better for BP IIs than BP Is because it seems to work better for depression than for mania.

Any of four types of psychotherapy may work especially well for bipolar patients:

- *Behavioral therapy:* For reducing stress
- *Cognitive therapy:* For identifying and changing patterns that may trigger mood swings
- *Cognitive-behavioral therapy (CBT):* For doing both of the above
- *Interpersonal therapy:* For working on relationships

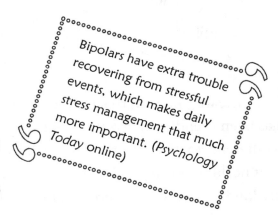

Bipolars have extra trouble recovering from stressful events, which makes daily stress management that much more important. (*Psychology Today* online)

Group therapy (see "Groupies: Good and [So, So] Bad" in this chapter) may also come into play at some point, along with support groups. Then there are social rhythm therapy, exposure therapy, family therapy, eye-movement desensitization and reprocessing (EMDR) therapy, light therapy, art and music therapy, animal-assisted therapy . . . none necessarily for bipolars, but not necessarily not. Which kind you try is up to you and your insurance.

Psychotherapy virgins may be nervous about what will happen when the door of the therapy room closes. Relax (preferably not on the couch; see "On/Off the Couch" in this chapter). Most likely, you'll sit in a comfortable chair facing the therapist, who won't be too close or too far away, and the first session will probably be Q&A. The therapist will ask most of the questions, leading you gently but deliberately along a path of diagnosis. Over time, as you develop mutual trust, the therapist may introduce new concepts and activities, all painless and all designed to help you.

> One of Freud's female patients supposedly tried to seduce him while she was lying on his couch. How Freudian is that?
> (BBC News Magazine)

I don't remember my first individual sessions with anyone but do recall some of the activities that came later: taking various exams (Chapter 10), including the infamous Rorschach ink-blot test; bringing Mom in for a session; and drawing a man and a woman. We'll draw a veil over therapy with my mother, but I must say that the therapist who asked for them enjoyed my man-and-woman drawings, which were stick figures. "This," he said happily, "is what we call the 'Fuck You Response.'" (I liked V. but didn't deny it.)

By the way, none of this hurt, caused embarrassment, or ended in tears. For me, talk therapy has been friendly conversation—*guided* conversation, but nothing alarming or exotic. If you have a different reaction, the therapist will almost certainly remind you that you're in a safe place and that nothing you say or do will leave the room. Both things will certainly be true. Most therapists are kind people who sincerely want to help their clients, including (and maybe especially) the ones who fear the process.

You needn't be afraid. No one will get Freudian unless your therapist is a Freudian or unless you do.

(Don't.)

Note: Psychotherapy can be expensive, especially if you don't have insurance or your policy has a sky-high deductible. Don't despair. Help is available. You can find a list of resources on the Mental Health America website at https://www.mhanational.org/paying-care. Also check Appendix B for organizations that can point you toward free or low-cost therapy.

The practice of lying on a psychiatrist's couch is largely mythical. Yes, it featured in a funny split-screen scene for Woody Allen and Diane Keaton in *Annie Hall*, and it's been the subject of many a *New Yorker* cartoon, but you'd be hard-pressed to find a horizontal patient in a modern psychiatry practice. Couch therapy was Freud's idea and, like so many other of his ideas, is out of fashion now.

For what it's worth, I've been in many psychiatrists' offices and never saw a couch in one until last winter. But Dr. M. has a large office that needs lots of furniture. He *has* lots. And I must say that the couch (which I sit on, thank you) is quite comfortable.

Still, no law says you can't lie down if your therapist has a couch and lying down would make you feel better. Freud himself was all for it; he said he didn't like clients staring at him all day. And who could blame him? Some of those people were *nuts*.

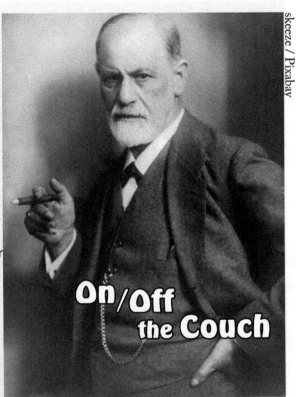

skeeze / Pixabay

On/Off the Couch

Zde / CC BY-SA 4.0 (Appendix C)

Freud's first therapy couch was a Victorian daybed—a gift from a woman he'd treated. (Read into that what you will.) Today, this groundbreaking furniture is in the Freud Museum in London. (*BBC News Magazine*)

P.S.: The shrink was on the cracked side himself. He believed (among other odd things) that analysis is always erotic and that only men are moral, for complicated reasons having to do with fear of castration. Guess that explains the cigar.*

* In all seriousness, Freud was addicted, smoking 20 or more cigars a day. He had 34 cancer surgeries in later life, according to the History Channel. But he never stopped smoking.

(What follows is an editorial of sorts. Feel perfectly free not to read it.)

Opinions differ. Many people adore group therapy and won't hear a word against it; others won't go near it except at gunpoint. My experience is necessarily subjective, but I'm happy to share the opinion that group can be both.

Groupies:
Good
and
(So, So) Bad

G o o d

The best group-therapy sessions I've ever had in were in hospitals. All the participants had bonded, which inevitably happens when people of similar ages and backgrounds are together 24/7. By design or osmosis, we knew and liked one another pretty well, including the therapist who led the sessions. Therefore, group therapy was respectful, helpful, and . . . well, therapeutic.

The catch is that you can get psychiatric-hospital group therapy only in a psychiatric hospital, so you have to be admitted, which is neither as easy nor as desirable as it may sound. I hope *you* do group on the outside.

B a d

Doing group on the outside is bad.

This is one opinion, of course. But snakes on a plane, look what *non*hospital group was like for me.

Perpetual drama   Almost every group has a dramatist. Take the young woman who gave us her Blanche DuBois for a whole session of one of my groups; this role worked so well for her that she encored the following week. (This Blanche was bogus, by the way; I'd seen real breakdowns by then.)

A good therapist would have shut her down after a few minutes to give the rest of us a chance for some therapy, which was what we were paying for. *That* therapist, however, let her monopolize all of both sessions, perhaps because it was less work that way. Whether Miss Neurotic Indiana gave a third performance is unknown; I quit the group after the second.

False advertising

During the mid-1990s, I was in individual therapy with an excellent therapist. Mrs. W. shared a building in the arts district with several other counselors, and like all districts of the type, it had flyers stapled to telephone poles up and down every block. One day after a session with Mrs. W., walking back to my car, I saw a new flyer for a workshop on a certain best-selling psychology book, led by another therapist in the same building.

How perfect was that? I'd liked the book, and here was a workshop about it in a place where I already went once a week.

Surprise! The workshop wasn't a workshop. It wasn't even about the book. It was ordinary group therapy except that all the other members were women, and the kind with whom I had nothing in common. This became evident at the very first session, when the therapist suggested a womb prayer (or some such burning absurdity) and I was the only one who laughed.

So much for that. I wasn't fooled twice by false advertising, but only because I'd been fooled once.

Offensive ennui

A few years later, after moving out of state and then back, I tried an outpatient clinic run by a hospital. The hospital wasn't the best, but its mental-health clinics were government-funded and offered the cheapest therapy around, so it couldn't hurt to try one.

Trying didn't hurt, not technically, but it seriously tested what little patience the gods and bipolar disorder gave me. This is how bad it was: I'd have to have two or three months of group therapy to get on a *waiting list* for individual therapy, but before I could get into a *group*, I'd have to have *individual therapy* with the counselor who led it. (Even today, this logic twists my bipolar brain.)

Was I on the hook for the cost of those unwanted sessions? You know the answer.

But I went to the first private session with the group leader anyhow. And I have to tell you, he was openly, insultingly bored through the whole of the hour. All he did was hand out page after page of photocopies, mostly of "cute" cartoons about therapy. Swear to God. I still have the only one that made me laugh: a man praying to be relieved of the totally unnecessary burdens he'd taken upon himself. Also swear to God: The counselor made eye contact for the first time only after I laughed and said, "At least you have a sense of humor." His tone added, "Not much of one."

Did he let me into his group? Dunno. I never went back.

Devious behavior

Was I being mean? Of course. I was an undiagnosed, constitutionally impatient bipolar pumped full of antidepressants and in no mood to be toyed with. Also (as mentioned in chapters 3 and 5), bipolar disorder and ADHD are cunning; they saw around the corners of group and showed me what was coming next. Besides, I'd had lots of experience with therapy groups by then and had a reasonable idea what to expect. Before long, I could tell when a thespian was about to take the stage (and whether there'd be real tears); what a lovelorn therapee was going to blame on his or her ex; and whether the therapist had, or wanted, any control. I could also judge to seconds when to call bullshit on someone—and often did, and rather enjoyed doing it.*

It was good to be the Antichrist of therapy. Perhaps it still is. You could sit me down in a group today, and I could tell the leader what he or she wanted to hear, the way he or she wanted to hear it, without a word of truth in it. This is not a skill I'm proud of.

You're likely to run into a manipulative jerk like me in group, which is one more reason why I recommend against it.

---

* I was almost certainly hypomanic at those times, feeling important, grandiose, and charmingly obnoxious. The *obnoxious* part of that last one was right.

If You Go . . .

Don't take my word entirely about group therapy, however. If your therapist recommends it and your budget allows, try giving group a go. Especially when you're in a depressive cycle, getting out of your head and into a circle of fellow sufferers can be a great help.

If you're lucky, you'll find a therapy group just for bipolars. Otherwise, you'll find a mixed group that you may love or hate. If you love it, great; keep going. If you don't, you can try another group or stick with individual counseling.

Just don't let the intake therapist test you with cartoons.

Our New Robot Overlords

geralt / Pixabay

I, for one, welcome them. So do some other bipolars, mostly the ones who haven't been helped enough by standard treatments. But fealty to machines is a personal choice.

Snark aside (for now), you have options beyond popping pills and talking to strangers. If you're OK with getting cozy with technology, you might check out these electromechanical marvels.

Electroconvulsive therapy (ECT)

Formerly known as *shock treatment*, the villain of such movies as *One Flew Over the Cuckoo's Nest* and *A Beautiful Mind*, ECT has come a long way since the bad old days. It still induces therapeutic seizures, but patients no longer have scary convulsions; they're given anticonvulsants first. (A finger or toe may twitch.) Neither are they awake when the seizures happen; nowadays, anesthesiologists give them a sedative.

ECT is said to work wonders for severe, treatment-resistant depression but knocks out memory something fierce. Most, if not all, comes back eventually, but some short-term memories may be gone for good.

I don't know why *causing* seizures is a good idea. Many BP IIs (like me) take *anti*seizure meds. But life is one big paradox, isn't it?

Vagus nerve stimulation (VNS)

The vagus nerve is the longest one in our craniums, going from brain to face to abdomen and affecting practically everything north of the feet: ears, thorax, pharynx, larynx, heart, lungs, stomach, gallbladder, pancreas, and many more. Why shooting electricity into this nerve helps severely depressed bipolars and unipolars is another mystery, but it *has* been known to work.

The shooting is done by a battery-powered implant in the chest. Apart from the surgery itself, side effects include sore throat and shortness of breath.

Cranial stimulation

For purposes of this discussion, there are two kinds: *transcranial magnetic stimulation* (TMS) and *cranial electrotherapy stimulation* (CES). Both involve placing small devices on the head that send electrical current through the brain. Bipolars may get TMS, which targets the mood-regulating parts of the brain; CES is most often used for depression, anxiety, and insomnia.

Biofeedback

Biofeedback as we know it has been around since the 1970s, the age of polyester, discos, and encounter groups. It may help bipolars; it may not. If you don't mind a machine beeping at you when your heart rate increases (as it might do when you're concentrating on holding it down), biofeedback could benefit you. It's supposed to be relaxing, at least—way more than the '70s generally.

Light therapy

It's not just for fixing screwed-up circadian rhythms or curing the winter blues. Light therapy (or *phototherapy*) may improve mood even in manic-depressives. For maximum safety and efficacy, experts recommend using a 10,000-lux box specifically designed for phototherapy. Also, use it with medical supervision, because too much light of this type can trigger hypomania (and mania).

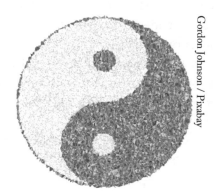

Gordon Johnson / Pixabay

Running and Walking and Sex, Oh My!

You go, beaches.

U.S. National Archives and Records Administration / public domain*

We're all overamped nowadays. That includes the 96 percent of adults who don't have ADHD. It certainly includes the 70 percent of manic-depressives who do (Chapter 5).

This isn't good. Stress is a well-known trigger of anxiety, which is a well-known trigger of mood swings in bipolars, especially BP IIs. Compounding the risk, anxiety and depression go together like tequila and lime, stressing bipolars even *more* during depressive cycles.

We need a vacation. Failing that, we need relief—say, running and walking and sex.

Don't let's jump right to the "sex" part. Quite a few G-rated practices are quality anxiolytics. All are (or can be) restful in their own ways, and we high-strung bipolars need all the rest we can get.

* The official title of this photo, taken on or around June 28, 1944, and reproduced here exactly, is *Mediterranean Beach Scene— Members of the Women's Army Corps stationed in North Africa. Recreational periods mean time off from the war.*

Aerobics, Etc.

Walking is good, and cheap too, depending on your taste in shoes. Almost everyone recommends it. Running also works (especially on a beach with your friends). But anything that gets your heart pumping will do. Consider:

- *Swimming:* Available year-round at your better-equipped health clubs and at high-school indoor pools (usually open to the public once a month or so). If you're not into swimming laps, you'll probably find water aerobics classes wherever you find pools.
- *Bicycling:* Good health clubs have lots of stationary bikes (upright and recumbent); some have spinning classes too. Or you can ride your own Specialized or Schwinn in the great outdoors—with a helmet, please, and reflective tape if you ride in the dark.
- *Rowing:* Why, yes, you can use the rowing machines at the club, but outdoor rowing is better, what with all that fresh air and the negative ions thrown off by moving water. You need access to some sort of craft, but there's such a thing as boat rental. As long as you stay away from whitewater and alligators, rowing can be a good hard stress-relieving workout.
- *Skating:* You probably roller-skated or rollerbladed back when. Try it again. Skating is like riding a bike, in that you never forget how. It's as much fun as you remember.

Easternish Breathing

An editorial director I know once taped the word BREATHE to her computer monitor, which has always struck me as being good advice. When you're stressed (and who isn't these days?), you're likely to breathe shallowly. Taking even one real hit of air will make you feel better. So, perhaps, will the following:

- *Tai chi:* The gentle stretching and deep breathing are calming and slooooooow. Often, tai chi is practiced outdoors, in parks and other pleasant settings, which is calming too.
- *Yoga:* It works for many people. Yoga can get a little woo-woo, but take it as exercise instead of religion, keep breathing no matter what, and you should be fine. Except for Triangle Pose.
- *Meditation:* This, too, works for many people. As bipolars, we may find it hard to concentrate—especially to concentrate on *not* concentrating—so meditation may be a challenge. Still, it never hurts to try to turn your brain off and breathe now and then.

Weirdish Noise

ASMR (autonomous sensory meridian response) is inexplicable to those who don't get it. Why, after all, would anyone listen on purpose to a person writing a letter, tapping a cup, raking sand, or narrating a pretend exam in a pretend doctor's office?

These examples are specific because I've listened to all of them, and many more. I *get* ASMR.

In a nutshell, ASMR induces deep relaxation along with a tingly, mildly electrical sensation—a mellow frisson, if you like. For those who can experience it, an everyday experience like a haircut can elicit it. But listening to specialized recordings is the easiest way to trigger the response because you don't need another person's input.

Try for yourself. Hundreds of podcasts, streams, and videos are as close as your favorite search engine. The videos may be extra-helpful because there's *also* such a thing as visual ASMR (see next).

> ASMR is a fairly specialized reaction. Studies estimate that only 40 percent of the population experiences ASMR, and only half of that 40 percent experiences it strongly.

Ear and Eye Candy

Certain videos and TV programs are inexplicably restful. Cooking shows, for example, work like magic for me. *The Great British Baking Show** is especially fine to watch. It's the small, repetitive motions of baking, I think, combined with friendly music and views of the grounds of a lovely English estate—an upscale nature video with puff pastry.

Then there's Bob Ross, whose shows are the quintessence of ASMR.

Ross hosted a half-hour program called *The Joy of Painting*, which ran from 1983 to 1994 on various public-television stations and is still available on PBS as *The Best of The Joy of Painting*. He had a remarkably hypnotic voice, and his painting technique matched it. A mic mounted close to the easel picked up every soft, pleasing sound, from the tap-tap-tap of a brush to the scrrrrrrape of the palette knife on canvas. Every episode is mesmerizing. And if you can go there with ASMR, Bob Ross can take you.

Those of us who can go there can testify that nothing is more relaxing. Well, almost nothing. Including . . .

---

* Known as *The Great British Bake-Off* across the water. I refer here only to the Mary Berry/Paul Hollywood, pre-2018 BBC version imported by PBS.

Sex

You didn't *really* think I was going to write about this. Of course it can be relaxing. It can be lots of things. Mostly, though, it's private.

Listening to Music

Soothing music is known to soothe the most savage. I've had luck with Enya, Tibetan singing bowls, and ambient chill; others prefer dulcimer or harp, which are also good; wind chimes can work. A scratchy recording of Beethoven's *Moonlight Sonata*** is an effective tranquilizer when played softly downstairs on a cold winter's night while you're warmly tucked into bed upstairs. And it's too bad that Windham Hill isn't around anymore, because its records were almost the definition of *laid-back*.

Whatever you find restful and relaxing, give it a spin when you need instant R&R. If Slayer calms you, who are we to judge?

Closely related to listening to music is . . .

Singing

You can sing in the shower. You can sing in the car. If you have a freestanding dwelling, thick walls, and hard-of-hearing neighbors, you can crank up the volume and sing all over the house.

Whatever genre floats your boat floats it, so if you like opera or EDM or show tunes, sing along. My favorites are New Wave and alternative, which don't always work a cappella, but you can generally sing, say, Green Day without Green Day.

Don't know the words? Who cares? If you like singing with R.E.M., you *have* to make up words because Michael Stipe's vocals can be inscrutable. Besides, it's fun to invent your own lyrics. Bastille's "Pompeii" is a favorite, for example, but I sing *octopus* for *optimist* now (it was a mistake the first time), and who will stop me?

And . . .

This list is necessarily partial, omitting handcrafts, birdwatching, acupuncture, and other placid pursuits. Whatever feels good, do it.

I'm serious about Bob Ross, though. His programs are instant Xanax, and I mean that nice. Don't believe me, just watch.

** In fact: Sonata no. 14 in C-sharp minor, *"quasi una fantasia,"* op. 27, no. 2.

Know Thyself Better

Being bipolar is only part of who you are. But how well do you know who that is?

Your sun sign doesn't count. Phrenology is phony. Psychic readings are bunk. You could read entrails, I suppose, or ask the Oracle at Delphi (but I've been there and didn't see her).

Maybe take a personality-type test?

The Internet is up to its HTML5 in free "who you are" quizzes. The following professional tests are far more accurate, however, so they're worth a thought and possibly worth the money:

- Milon Clinical Multiaxial Inventory (MCMI)
- Minnesota Multiphasic Personality Inventory (MMPI)
- Myers-Briggs Type Indicator (Myers-Briggs or MBTI)
- Riso-Hudson Enneagram Type Indicator (RHETI)
- Strong Interest Inventory (acronym-free)

Some people call Myers-Briggs a vocational horoscope. Each to his or her own opinion, of course, but some people have nailed their minds shut. I took both Myers-Briggs and Strong (then called Strong-Campbell) at a therapist's office in 1987 and still have the results, which align perfectly with those of every other type test I've taken—including some weird thing that a former boss forced on the whole staff. All these results were, and still are, scary-accurate.

The official tests aren't free and are offered only in psychologists' and psychotherapists' offices. Still, they may be worthwhile. The results may add another dimension to your picture of who you are, which might help you see your bipolar diagnosis from a more-complex, less-overwhelming perspective. For more information on testing, ask your therapist or check the websites listed in Appendix B.

> The Myers-Briggs types (you lean toward one in each pair) are Extroverted/Introverted, *Sensing/Intuitive,* Thinking/Feeling, and Judging/Perceiving. *Introverted*, by the way, doesn't mean *shy*; introverts simply need alone time to recharge their batteries.

Even better (to my mind) is archetypal psychology, devised by Carl Gustav Jung and popularized by his student James Hillman. The theory behind it holds that each person's psyche contains distinct myth-informed personae called *archetypes* and that these archetypes drive personality. The number of archetypes depends on the archetypal psychologist (some say six, some say twelve, one says both), and the names may differ, but the personae are recognizably the same because they're drawn from universal myth.

Dr. Carol S. Pearson, for example, has written about twelve archetypes that represent stages in a life's journey and that circle back on themselves:*

Innocent	Caregiver/Martyr	Destroyer	Magician
Orphan	Seeker/Wanderer	Creator	Sage
Warrior	Lover	Ruler	Fool

The concept of the circular journey—origin as destination—is ancient, Eastern, *and* Western clear back to Odysseus. It appeals to me strongly. We bipolars necessarily live closer to our psyches than the average person does, so even though manic-depression isn't our whole identity, I think it impels us to find out what else goes on inside. But if archetypal psychology isn't your thing, never mind.

By the way, if there's a bipolar myth, I say it's the Myth of Sisyphus (Chapter 11).

* It can't be a coincidence that twelve is the number of Jungian archetypes *and* the number of Olympian gods and goddesses. However many there are, you can self-test to see how active (or inactive) they are in your life. Those with the imagination of a doorknob may disapprove, but I've found my archetypal makeup to be accurate, relevant, useful, and fun.

stux / 7228 / pixabay

Chapter 11

Living While Bipolar

Nobody said life is easy. But we all wish somebody would. In this day and age, just making it through the 365/24/7 can be murder; add bipolar disorder, and the murder can feel premeditated.

Being bipolar when most people aren't is exceptionally challenging. We manic-depressives are different. We can be difficult. *Predictable* is a word in the dictionary. For BP IIs especially, so is *impervious*. We often feel like strangers in this world, which is peopled mainly by cheerful, aggressive, thick-skinned, conventional, team-player lifeforms who seem alien to us, who keep telling us that we're too sensitive, or idealistic, or moody, or emotional.

Well, I've got two words for them and maybe for you: *So what?*

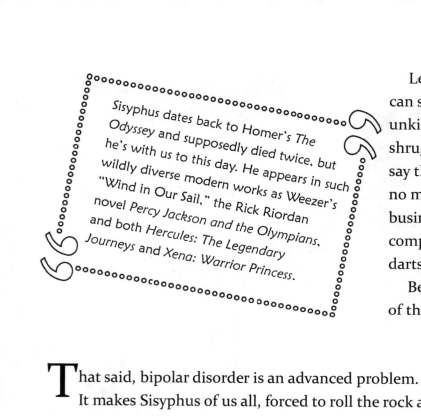

Sisyphus dates back to Homer's *The Odyssey* and supposedly died twice, but he's with us to this day. He appears in such wildly diverse modern works as Weezer's "Wind in Our Sail," the Rick Riordan novel *Percy Jackson and the Olympians*, and both *Hercules: The Legendary Journeys* and *Xena: Warrior Princess*.

Learn these words. Love them. Use them. You can say them kindly if the accuser isn't being unkind—only clueless or dim—but feel free to shrug and smile an infuriating smile when you say them to a clod. Life is short. Your life is *yours*, no matter how your brain works, and it's no one's business how sensitive you are, let alone how complicated. If you and I aren't "normal," tough darts.

Besides, normal is overrated. You've *seen* some of those people, right?

That said, bipolar disorder is an advanced problem. It's exacting and exhausting. It's never over. It makes Sisyphus of us all, forced to roll the rock and roll the rock and roll the rock uphill. Every now and then, we get crushed when the inevitable happens.

Life is especially hard for bipolars. That's just how it is.

But even hard lives have a funny way of evening out, because our particular challenges have peculiar compensations. After all, getting through day after day while confused, upset and/or scared, manic/hypomanic, depressive, or in a mixed state takes much more strength than most nonbipolars have.

So try to think of this disorder as a different kind of gift. No one wants to keep rolling that rock up this hill, but on a clear day, you can see forever from here.

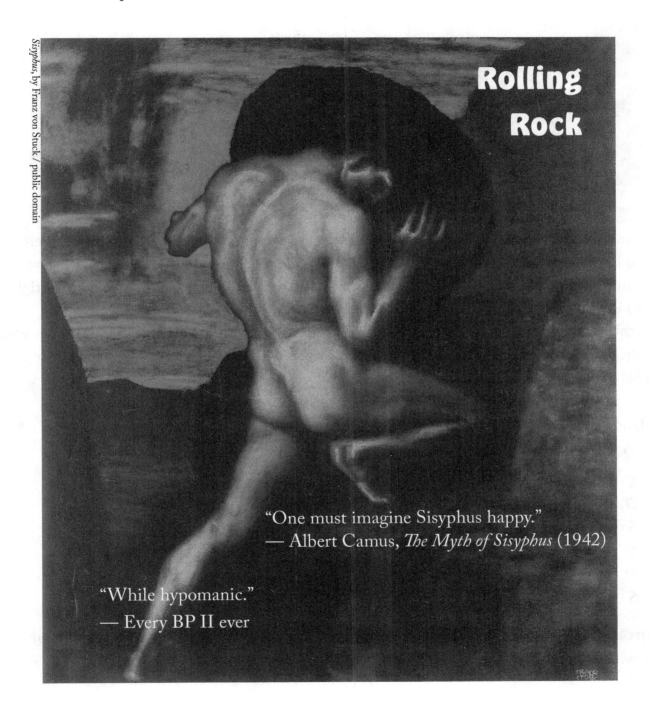

Rolling Rock

"One must imagine Sisyphus happy."
— Albert Camus, *The Myth of Sisyphus* (1942)

"While hypomanic."
— Every BP II ever

Should I Say or Should I No?

Coming out as bipolar, as it were, isn't like that other coming out. There are no closets, there are no laws against it, and only the judgiest loony would protest it. (On the downside, we have no recognizable bipolar culture, including cool music, and we should do something about that right away.) But bipolars still have to choose whether to tell, and whom.

Ideally, everyone in your life is perfect and perfectly happy with you all the time, no matter what. *Ideally,* mocha lattes are health food and kale smoothies are punishable. These scenarios being unlikely, you'll have to make some decisions.

You may want (or need) to keep your disorder secret, in which case never mind.

If, however, you want to talk, there are better and worse reasons and ways to go about it.

R e a s o n s

- *Worse:* Wanting attention
- *Better:* Seeking support
- *Worse:* Getting even ("You made me bipolar!")
- *Better:* Giving reassurance ("It's not your fault!")
- *Worse:* Blaming everything on your illness
- *Better:* Taking responsibility for your own unforced nonbipolar errors

In other words, do convey information; don't play the world's smallest (or largest) violin for yourself just because you have this thing.

W
a
y
s

- *Worse:* Making a general announcement at a class reunion
- *Better:* Telling a small group of trusted people to start with
- *Worse:* Posting the news on Facebook or (really worse) Twitter
- *Better:* Telling a small group of trusted people to start with
- *Worse:* Having KISS ME, I'M MANIC-DEPRESSIVE printed on a T-shirt
- *Better:* Telling a small group of trusted people to start with

You get the drift. Start small. Keep your friends close. Stay *way* off social media unless you like being trolled.

OK, you've talked to the people closest to you—say, relatives, friends, and/or tennis partners. Who next?

Perhaps no one. No one has to know everything. Or maybe no one else has to right now. The bipolar talk isn't eggs; it won't expire.

Finally, you should decide whether to tell anyone outside your inner circle. Your circumstances will vary from everyone else's, of course, and so will your decisions. But here are a few suggestions:

Your significant other (first, if you're smart)
The human-resources department at work if/when you have to
Your boss, if your illness affects your attendance or job performance*
All your medical-care providers

Facebook friends you don't know well
Anyone who has ever offered to tell you what's wrong with you
Your brand-new and/or monstrous, feral boss who runs on all fours

Your Facebook friends list *on* Facebook
Frenemies
Anyone you don't like much
Your least-discreet friend or relative

Your priest, minister, imam, rabbi, guru, or New Age leader
A fellow manic-depressive whom you know to be manic-depressive *and* open about it**
Your barber and/or hairstylist, because you probably tell him or her everything anyway

Some people say that pets are people too, so if you feel the need to tell yours, do that. Dogs especially make excellent listeners and never judge. (Cats, not so much. And never trust a lizard.)

* You don't have to say that your illness is bipolar disorder. But talk to HR to be sure of your rights under federal employment law (see "Bipolar Pride—and Prejudice" in this chapter).

** Only when you're both well, or reasonably so.

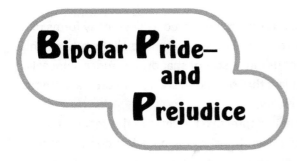

Bipolar Pride— and Prejudice

In this book, I've talked about being bipolar in a fairly light way. That's not because this disorder is any laughing matter; it's because so many bipolars are so afraid of it. My thesis here is that bipolarity isn't always as bad as some citizens of Bipolar Nation think. It's an illness, but an illness with benefits. We didn't choose it (who would?), but we can choose to embrace what it gives us: endurance, empathy, deep experience, complex understanding, and a taste for the black comedy of life. Even if we can't go so far as to be proud of being bipolar, we shouldn't be ashamed. Our disorder stems from brain chemistry. It's medical. *Why do you think we take meds?*

On the flip side (there's always a flip side in manic depression), our gifts come with forfeits, such as mood cycles, medication, side effects, confusion, and—perhaps the greatest of these—discrimination.

You really can't blame normals for not understanding. More complex than plain depression or anxiety, less overt than schizophrenia, inexplicable in its changes, and incurable by its nature, bipolar disorder is a mystery to most nonbipolars. They can't figure it out. We can't always explain it. In some ways, we live in a foreign country and may not be welcome to cross the border. Manic depression might be catching!

Twaddle. The worst. But even sophisticated, rational people may think that way on some level. Human brains are built on lizard brains, and you know how lizard people are.*

Reptilian thinking guides too many people who are scared of mental illness, which is too many people. There's no law against scared. But there *are* laws against discrimination. We bipolars and all others with mental illnesses have certain rights, including informed consent about treatment, freedom to live where we choose, and confidentiality of our mental-health records. (There are exceptions in the case of court orders, but I'm talking here about the usual.)

What's more, a couple of federal laws are designed to protect our jobs:

- *Americans with Disabilities Act (ADA):* This 1990 law was amended in 2008 to include bipolar disorder. It protects disabled people (including bipolars) against discrimination at work, provided that they meet certain criteria.
- *Family and Medical Leave Act (FMLA):* Signed into law in 1993, the FMLA gives bipolars and other people with serious health conditions the right to take up to 12 weeks' leave in a year, again with certain conditions. (See "Breaking Away" in this chapter.)

Most states also have mental-health statutes that spell out certain rights.

> Insane isn't a medical term; it's a legal one. The word doesn't even appear in DSM-5. But crazy does (descriptively only). (The Week online)

Under the law, then, we're protected against many forms of discrimination. Beyond the law, we often face all the others. This fact forces some of us into a sort of shadow existence, concealing our illness, pretending that our mood swings are ordinary moods, denying our very reality.

Every single manic-depressive has lived in the shadows. Laws or no laws, we don't want to risk being fired. We don't want to be called crazy to our faces or behind our backs. We'd rather not tell friends and family members, who might disapprove. And who would marry, date, or swipe right on us if they knew?

I don't have any answers, having been deep undercover myself and even now being ambivalent about letting the secret out. No bipolar can help being bipolar, but it's easy to be ashamed even of what we can't help.

Still, I'm fighting that impulse—not all the way to pride but halfway to owning the illness. Maybe you can get there too.

---

* I know them mostly from sci-fi and profoundly hope that they never take over. Even though Douglas Adams said they already have.**

** He said this in *So Long, and Thanks for All the Fish*, Book 4 of *The Hitchhiker's Guide to the Galaxy* series (Ballantine Books/Del Rey, 2005).***

*** I love it, but then, of course, I'm manic-depressive.

> Some researchers think that depression and prejudice are intimately linked. It's depressing for anyone to experience prejudice, of course. But often, the prejudice is self-directed: depressives against themselves. (*Perspectives on Psychological Science* and PsychCentral)

It's no news that medicine has a white-male bias. From roughly the '50s to the early '90s, young white men were considered to be the benchmark of the species, so they were the primary subjects of research and clinical trials. Even today, even unconsciously, many doctors in all specialties treat patients based on that outdated model.

Some of those doctors, of course, treat bipolar patients.

There are more than a few problems with gender-biased medicine. For one, the U.S. population breaks down this way nowadays, according to *The Washington Post*:*

Handle with Care: particular Populations

- White women: 32 percent
- White men: 31 percent
- Nonwhite men: 19 percent
- Nonwhite women: 19 percent

Some women of all races and some nonwhite men have bipolar disorder.

For another, a 2017 Gallup poll found that 4.5 percent of Americans identify as LGBTQ+.

Some of them have bipolar disorder.

Finally, the 2010 U.S. Census reported that 13 percent of Americans are 65 and older, a figure that's expected to rise to 20 percent by 2020.

You know what some of them have.

We bipolars are diverse. Our treatment ought to be too.

In *Bipolar Disorder For Dummies*, Dr. Candida Fink and Joe Kraynak list several characteristics that are more common in bipolar women than in bipolar men:

- Depression
- BP II diagnosis
- Mixed episodes
- Rapid cycling
- Later onset
- Comorbid conditions, both psychiatric and medical
- Medication-induced weight gain

And (of course)

- Pregnancy
- Menarche, menses, and menopause

Furthermore, many women take oral contraceptives, which may not get on well with bipolar meds.

All these situations absolutely require special care. Bipolar women who are pregnant, nursing, or taking birth-control pills may need less or different medication. Also, a great many women fear weight gain, which is a side effect of some psychoactive drugs. Doctors should take this fear seriously and treat it sensitively, because some women (and men) will stop taking *any* medication that adds 5, 10, or 15 pounds—or more.

People in every ethnic group the world over have bipolar disorder. But ethnicity can affect reactions to medication. Fink and Kraynak note that African-Americans and Asians tend to metabolize some drugs slowly, whereas Ethiopians, Ethiopian and Sephardic Jews, and Arabs may be "ultra-rapid metabolizers." Metabolize a med too slowly, and serum levels of the drug become too high, potentially increasing side effects; metabolize too fast, and serum concentrations may not reach therapeutic levels.

Another potential problem: Cultural norms may affect bipolars' willingness to seek treatment because some cultures stigmatize mental illness more than others do.

Ethnic Groups

Seniors

All over-65s, bipolar and otherwise, process medication differently from younger people—including their younger selves. They may require smaller doses or different medications. Frankly, they may be overmedicated: A study cited in *The Washington Post* estimated that 25 percent of people ages 65 to 69, and 40 percent of those 70 to 79, take at least five prescription drugs.

When it comes to psychiatric medications, the percentage of seniors who take at least three of them has more than doubled in recent years. It's hard to imagine that all this mental-health medication *wouldn't* mess with mental health.

Also (and unavoidably when you're talking about this age group), doctors have to be on the watch for Alzheimer's and other dementias, which can overlap with and worsen bipolar symptoms.

LGBTQ+

LGBTQ+ bipolars often face double discrimination. The extra stress can trigger mood cycles, making the moods worse.

It would be nice to think otherwise, but even some doctors may be biased against them. (Prejudice itself doesn't discriminate.)

Then there's the special challenge of transgender hormone therapy, which induces a second puberty, often complete with mood swings. Even stable transgender bipolars are at risk of coming unbalanced under these circumstances, so they should tell their prescribers about the HRT.

If any of these categories includes you and/or a bipolar loved one, never assume that mental-health professionals know. (You can't tell anything just by looking.) Specific populations of bipolars really *do* need to be handled with care.

Note: You can find more information about mental health care for diverse populations at https://www.nami.org/Find-Support/Diverse-Communities.

* If you're checking the math, these figures add up to 101 percent; presumably, rounding occurred somewhere.

Breaking Away

Sometimes, even with the best treatment, bipolar disorder goes bad. Stressful life events, medication changes, downturns in physical health—all these things (and others) can bring more pressure to bear than manic-depressives can reasonably stand. Under that pressure, private and work lives may crack.

Here's what you can do about work.

The good news is that your boss can't fire you or otherwise discriminate against you for being bipolar, much less for getting worse. By law, according to the U.S. Equal Employment Opportunity Commission (EEOC), you're entitled to reasonable accommodation for mental-health conditions that "substantially limit" your functionality. Bipolar disorder is listed as one of those conditions, and the EEOC website says you should "easily qualify" (underlining theirs) for such accommodation. Talk to your supervisor or the human resources department about your options.

If accommodation fails, and you're so seriously impaired that you can't do your job, you may be able to make a clean break for a while. The FMLA (see "Bipolar Pride—and Prejudice" in this chapter) allows you to take up to 12 weeks of leave in a year, and depending on your employer's policy, you may be able to keep drawing your pay while you're away.

There's a catch, of course: Both you and your employer have to qualify under U.S. Department of Labor (DoL) rules. The agency lists these conditions (simplified here for overview purposes):

Employers
- Must be private-sector with 50 or more employees, or
- public-sector with any number of employees, or
- a public or private school (elementary or secondary) with any number of employees

Employees
- Must work for a covered employer
- Must have worked at least 1,250 hours for the employer in the past 12 months (not necessarily consecutively)
- Must work at a location where the employer has at least 50 employees within a 75-mile radius

Qualifying reasons for taking leave under the FMLA, DoL says, include "a serious health condition that makes the employee unable to perform the essential functions of his or her job"—and mental illness counts.

The law is on your side. If you qualify for FMLA leave and you need it, *take* it.

Full disclosure #2: A few months after President Bill Clinton signed the act into law, I was hospitalized again (briefly), and my employer's HR director encouraged me to take FMLA leave to recover. This leave was a godsend, given my shaky mental state, and I was lucky enough to work for a company that paid my salary the whole time.

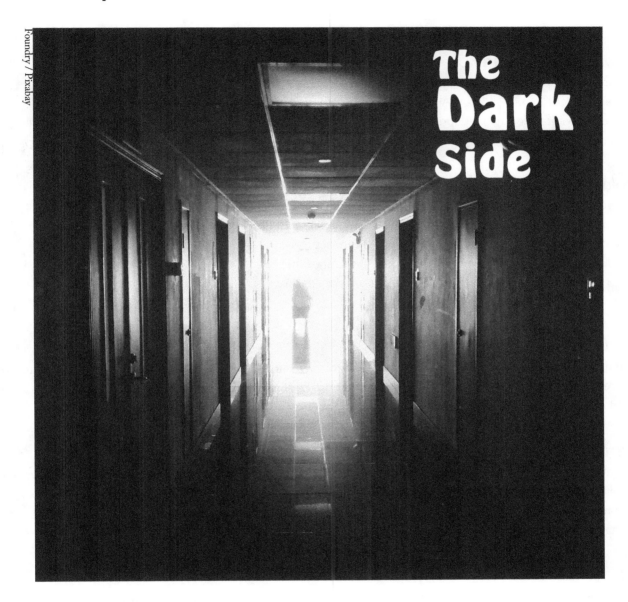

The Dark Side

Foundry / Pixabay

Like most things, bipolar disorder has a dark side. This book has discussed mostly benign experiences and good outcomes so far, but I'm well aware that we're all one extreme mood cycle from disaster.

The reasons are many.

Comorbidities (Chapter 5)

Substance abuse frequently co-occurs with bipolar disorder, but it can land *anyone* in rehab, detox, Alcoholics Anonymous, a halfway house, or a hospital. For manic-depressive substance abusers, the risk is compounded by bipolar medications and mood swings.

Bipolar depression (Chapter 7)

As you're tired of hearing by now if you've read in order, bipolar depression is different from and worse than the unipolar kind. BP IIs, whose cycles are weighted heavily toward depression, are usually down deeper and more severely than BP Is and nonbipolars, not to mention longer—even for years. Our depressions are debilitating. Our risk of suicide is high.

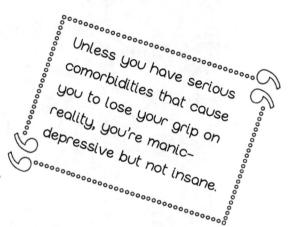

Unless you have serious comorbidities that cause you to lose your grip on reality, you're manic-depressive but not insane.

Destructive relationships (Chapter 12)

BP IIs are supersensitive to rejection—so much so that we may turn on loved ones before they turn on us. We may even *expect* them to turn on us. This mindset isn't the least bit healthy; taken to extremes and/or in an already-fraught relationship, it can be dangerous.

Destructive lives (Chapter 3)

Many bipolars have trouble doing what most people do every day as a matter of routine. We can't always hold jobs. Bills may stack up because we don't have the money to pay them or can't be bothered while depressed. It may be too much trouble to see family and friends, who understandably don't understand, which can torch relationships. Personal hygiene may go by the wayside, which rarely helps relationships either.

Abuse (Chapter 12)

For whatever reason—frustration, fear, sense of rejection—a few manic-depressives act out violently. The details are different in every case, but they're all the worst kind of bad news.

Bipolarity isn't a marker of violence or victimhood, but bipolars are at increased risk of the latter. Studies cited by the NCBI found that (a) men and women with bipolar disorder are eight times more likely to experience domestic violence than those who don't have mental disorders and that (b) over a lifetime, an estimated 26.7 percent of bipolar women and 7.1 percent of bipolar men are assaulted by domestic partners.

Even taking bipolar disorder out of the equation, the danger is shockingly common. The National Coalition Against Domestic Violence says that in the United States alone, 20 people are abused by intimate partners *every minute*—an aggregate 10 million assaults every year. Further, 1 in 3 women and 1 in 4 men have been assaulted by domestic partners, many of them seriously (1 in 4 women and 1 in 9 men).

The news is no better when you factor in the LGBTQ+ community. A 2010 study by the Centers for Disease Control and Prevention (CDC) found that among women, 61 percent of bisexuals, 44 percent of lesbians, and 35 percent of heterosexuals have experienced partner violence, stalking, and/or rape. Among men, 37 percent of bisexuals, 29 percent of heterosexuals, and 26 percent of gays have been victims.

Whatever your hangups and mine, we surely have one in common: an unhealthy obsession with our smartphones. You might call it phone sex except that it just barely isn't. Whatever twisted stuff goes on in the latest pay-TV smash, you can bet that 99 percent of viewers will watch it while fooling around with their phones and that 100 percent of that 99 percent would rather sleep with their gizmos.

Tell me you don't sleep with your phone on the nightstand, under your pillow, maybe *on* your pillow. Or that you don't spend more time interacting with it than with most of the real people in your real world.

Look, I'm as every bit as guilty. Like you, I've sat at crowded lunch and dinner tables with no conversation because all of us were busy with phones. This behavior isn't healthy, especially for manic-depressives. Why?

Relationships with phones are one-way.

We bipolars are challenged enough in human relationships. It can't be good for us to invest so much of our limited time, energy, and libido in a slab of plastic, metal, and smudgy glass that gives us nothing in return. (Facebook notifications *do not count*.)

Relationships with phones are inexplicable.

The New York Times cites a University of Maryland study of smartphone users in ten countries, a third of whom said they'd give up sex before they'd give up their phones. Would you? And how would you explain that choice to your significant other (assuming that you still have a significant other ten seconds later)?

Relationships with phones are distracting.

Not only in the don't-drive-while-texting sense (but *don't* do that). Even without comorbid ADHD, bipolars can be easily distracted, especially during manic/hypomanic cycles, and smartphones are designed to distract. The *NYT* reported in 2017 that smartphone owners checked their phones 150 times a day—every 9.6 minutes! That figure has to be higher today.

Relationships with phones are impulsive.

You know what hypomania is like. You also know what smartphones are like. The combination can be disastrous when your credit card and favorite shopping app interact; when you swipe right on a fishy person; when you decide to hire long-distance ride sharing, book transcontinental flights, reserve grand-hotel suites, and do other unaffordable spur-of-the-moment things. What's more, stalkery things can happen to you on social media if you let your guard down and let them.

Relationships with phones mess with sleep.

The WHO cites studies that found changes in smartphone users' brain activity, including their sleep patterns. Although the organization calls these effects "minor," tell that to a wired manic bipolar who's already been up for a day or two. Heavy phone use can't possibly help.

Moreover, study after study has found that the blue light emitted by smartphones plays havoc with sleep. iPhones have a Night Shift feature that let users customize this light, shifting it from blue to the desired degree of yellow at specified times. Still, even Apple engineers must know that it would be better to put the phone in a drawer at bedtime (or turn it off altogether).

> Count each day as a
> separate life.
> — Seneca

Relationships with phones could kill you.

Well, maybe not. But maybe:

- If you use your phone while driving, your chances of crashing are three to four times higher.
- Researchers are looking into links between mobile phones and brain tumors.
- A smartphone used too close to a medical device (such as a pacemaker) can seriously interfere with that device.

Relationships with phones never end.

I've had iPhones since the 3GS and have mostly loved them, but lately, owning one has been like owning a Tamagotchi—one of those bizarre digital pets that were big in the late 1990s and early 2000s. You couldn't ignore those plastic pests; if you didn't "feed" them, they "died." Likewise, most mornings now, three or four apps want updating, or some social-media platform wants attention, which is the phone's way of needing to be "fed" so it won't "die."

What a nuisance! Especially when depressed, we bipolars don't always take great care of ourselves, so how can we parent a needy phone that will never leave home?

All that said, I'm in too deep with mine to give it up yet, but this relationship isn't working, and any day now, I'm going to break up. *Hang* up, anyway.

You go first. No, you.

> May you have the hindsight to know where you've been,
> The foresight to know where you are going,
> And the insight to know when you have gone too far.
> — Irish blessing

411 withOUT 911

To live your very best bipolar life, you need allies: friends, family, and partners, to be sure, but also trained professionals. Here are a few options of the fourth kind that you may encounter.

Psychiatrists

Like all other medical doctors, psychiatrists go to med school, complete residency, and earn M.D. degrees; some also have Ph.D.s. Being doctors, they can prescribe and manage medication as well as treat psychiatric conditions. You may find a few who also offer individual counseling, but the cost per session may be high.

You're most likely to be referred to a psychiatrist by your family doctor, a hospital doctor (if you're about to be discharged from a hospital), or a therapist.

Therapists

Therapists come in whole constellations, with varying types of licenses from state to state. Wherever you live, you're likely to have a choice among the following:

- *Psychologists:* Like psychiatrists, psychologists are medical doctors, but their degrees are Ph.D. or Psy.D. instead of M.D. Some have M.S. degrees and work under doctoral supervision. All can diagnose but can't prescribe. Psychologists specialize in testing and in counseling, both individual and group (Chapter 10).
- *Psychotherapists:* Look for a licensed, degreed (M.S. or M.A.) counselor, clinician, or therapist. All three terms mean essentially the same thing, but these therapists usually have certain specialties, including marriage or family therapy and substance abuse.
- *Psychiatric mental-health nurses:* These nurses have a master's degree or doctorate as well as an R.N. license. Those with advanced degrees (such as Ph.D. or Ed.D.) often work as psychotherapists; in some states, they're nurse practitioners who can prescribe and oversee medication. You'll find psychiatric nurses in hospitals, outpatient clinics, and private practice.
- *Licensed clinical social workers (LCSWs) and clinical social workers:* As the titles imply, these therapists have MSW degrees; LCSWs also complete post-master's coursework and pass state licensure exams. Like psychotherapists, LCSWs and clinical social workers have various specialties in addition to training in evaluation, therapy, and case management.

- *Social workers:* They're not quite the same as clinical social workers and are more likely to provide case management and various planning and placement services. They have B.A. or B.S. degrees instead of MSWs.
- *Pastoral counselors:* Pastoral counselors are (as you might expect) members of the clergy who have special training in counseling.

No one type of therapist is better than another; specialties and services vary. Choose the kind that best fits your needs. If your insurance or bank account permits, it's ideal to have a psychiatrist (or psychiatric nurse practitioner) to handle your medication and a counselor to provide some sort of therapy.

As to where to find a therapist, you might call the nearest hospital for a referral. Better yet, ask a few close, trusted people for suggestions. With luck, a highly recommended therapist will still be accepting new patients and won't cost the sun and the moon. Best case, he or she will take your insurance. (You'll be out of pocket the whole fee otherwise, so be sure to ask.)

Support Groups

If you live in or near a city of any size, support groups should be thick on the ground. Most cities have numerous mental-health programs, both public and private, as well as hospitals with mental-health departments (often called *behavioral care*). A therapist should be able to refer you to a local support group if he or she doesn't offer one.

For those who live in a small town or rural zip code, the challenge is greater. Apart from having fewer options for support, these places can be notoriously short on privacy, making visits to a therapist's office more public than necessary.

These organizations can hook you up with online and local support groups:

- *NAMI:* Call the HelpLine at (800) 950-6264 or visit https://www.nami.org/Find-Support.
- *Depression and Bipolar Support Alliance:* The DBSA's website is at www.DBSAlliance.org.
- *Mental Health America:* Support info is on the MHA website at www.mentalhealthamerica.net.

trevoykellyphotography / Pixabay

gracinistudios / Pixabay

You got to have friends.*
—Bette Midler

LuckyLife11 / Pixabay

Spiritze / Pixabay

chezbeate / Pixabay

Anita_Morgan / Pixabay

* "Friends," from *Bette Midler* (Atlantic Records, 1973).

Part 5

Seven Stories

(Plus One)

We're almost done here, so let's end with seven stories about bipolar disorder and then my last word. *Caution:* Some of what follows is disturbing. All of it is true.

Friends, Family, and/or Loved Ones: Relationship Roulette

L.
Formerly married

How long did you know him before you found out he was bipolar?

About eight years.

Did you suspect it before you found out? If so, why?

No, but A. had bouts of depression and couldn't pull himself out. He told me he thought about suicide daily. He thought that was normal.

He also went on strange buying sprees. We had at least 100 rolls of toilet paper in the house at all times, and he and the kids always had to have the newest tennis shoes.

How did he find out that he's bipolar?

I'm a school counselor, so I knew about most mental illnesses. Then I did some research on bipolar disorder and talked him into seeing our family doctor, who diagnosed him. The doctor didn't want to treat him, but A. refused to see a psychiatrist.

The doctor treated him for several years with several drugs, which weren't very successful, and finally talked him into seeing a psychiatrist to get the proper med combo.

Do you know what kind of bipolar diagnosis he has?

BP I. The doctor was surprised he was able to hold a job.

Did you know anything about bipolar disorder before he was diagnosed?

I knew about the extreme highs and lows, and I knew mania can manifest in many ways. [His mania was] getting angry and going on spending sprees.

Were you able to tell when he was in a manic/hypomanic or depressive cycle?

He was angry when he was depressed. When he was manic, he was hypersexual. He bought books and wanted to try different positions; he wanted to role-play. I don't believe he ever cheated on me, although I wouldn't be surprised.

Were you ever afraid of his behavior?

Not physically afraid. He was very emotionally abusive. Twice, I had enough and tried to get him to hit me so I'd have a good reason to divorce him. But he never hit me. It was all emotional abuse.

A. acted out in public too. He'd get angry and aggressive with other people. I wasn't afraid he would hit someone, but he made a spectacle of himself with his rages and embarrassed the family. I always had to tiptoe around him and deflect his moods to protect the children.

I don't think all of his behavior was due to bipolar disorder; he also had some nasty learned behaviors. I'm not sure he ever learned how to treat family with respect.

What do you wish you'd known then about bipolar disorder? What do you wish you know now?

I doubt I would have changed much, because I wouldn't have had my son and daughter if we hadn't married. But I wish I'd had the power to help him deal with his illness better. I wish I'd known how to make him go to therapy and get the help he needed.

What advice would you give anyone else who's close to a bipolar person?

Because I'm a counselor, I've helped several couples find therapists and psychiatrists that they were comfortable with. I think therapy is important for people who are involved with bipolars. If one person in a couple has a mental illness, it affects the family as a whole.

Do you have any suggestions about what to say or not to say to a bipolar?

I was always open and honest with A., but he had triggers. If I told him he was acting paranoid, for example, that always lit him up. When a person with bipolar disorder manifests anger, it's difficult to know what to say, but you probably shouldn't say things that you know might trigger episodes.

Anything else you'd like to add?

I fully believe that if people with bipolar disorder are properly medicated and want to be better, they can be. Some people may not need counseling after they understand their illness and how it affects them, but other people will. Each person is different. Each illness is different.

J.
Currently married

How long did you know her before you found out she's bipolar?

We graduated together, reconnected in 2014, and married in January 2016. I found out about her past mental health issues on our first anniversary.

Did you suspect it before you found out? If so, why?

I knew something was slightly off, but when I found out, the pieces came together.

How did she find out that she's bipolar?

She was diagnosed with severe anxiety many years ago and was given medication. No counseling treatment plan was done, although there were discussions of her being an outpatient in a mental health facility. At that time, the psychiatrist suggested that she also suffered from mild levels of bipolar disorder, but since she dropped all treatment plans, there was no follow-up.

Do you know what kind of bipolar diagnosis she has?

Based on what I have been able to gather, the doctor was suggesting BP II.

Did you know anything about bipolar disorder before she was diagnosed?

I only knew what most people knew, which was mostly incorrect or slanted, depending on who was describing it.

Are you able to tell when she's in a manic/hypomanic or depressive cycle?

In the manic cycle, she begins to make outlandish statements, often very hateful, which goes 180 degrees counter to her normal disposition. She also seems to have altered sleep patterns, as well as distinct changes in appetite. Based on her normal personality behaviors, she doesn't appear as what most would consider manic, which is why it was difficult for those not around her for significant periods of time to notice these changes.

Have you ever been afraid of her behavior?

No, although oftentimes, there are moments of extreme rage, which is—again—opposite of her typical behavior.

What do you wish you'd known earlier about bipolar disorder? What do you wish you know now?

I wish I had known earlier about her particular issues, which went unchecked and unmanaged for too many years. I have done extensive research on various mental health disorders, which has given me a better understanding. However, my wish now would be that she accept her issues and willingly participate in some treatment plan.

What advice would you give anyone else who's close to a bipolar person?

I think the best resource to help anyone would be knowledge—not just about bipolar, but about other disorders that may [affect] acknowledging, understanding, and treating someone with this disorder.

Do you have any suggestions about what to say or not to say to a bipolar?

I think that is a very difficult thing to answer, based on what I have found in my own research; each patient presents differently, and there is no cookie-cutter solution. I know that when I approached my wife to discuss these issues, she was very defensive and for several weeks continued to deny that she was bipolar, often turning to mocking, diverting the topic, or refusing to discuss it at all.

It was like going through the five stages of grief or loss: 1. Denial and isolation; 2. Anger; 3. Bargaining; 4. Depression; and 5. Acceptance. But with [my] calm persistence, extreme patience, and showing [her] documents and articles one at a time over a period of about two weeks, she finally began to accept that she needed to seek help.

Unfortunately, that hasn't occurred yet.

Anything else you'd like to add?

I think the one thing I have learned about various mental health disorders is that we can't be too quick to slap on a diagnosis.

With another family member, there was an initial diagnosis that was changed several months later, and no additional testing or attempts at diagnosing ever took place. At that point, he was so overmedicated that with 12 different medications, there were 32 drug interactions, most categorized as severe or significant. He was sleeping nearly 20 hours a day, but since the psychiatrist

who managed his treatment for many years had told the family that he was "as good as he would ever be" in terms of his behaviors and activities, they simply ignored what was happening.

It was through an introduction to this person that I began doing extensive research, much of it including bipolar and other significant behavioral disorders.

B.
Formerly engaged

How long did you know him before you found out that he was bipolar?

He was diagnosed before I met him, but being a typical bipolar, he had formulated this persona in order to charm someone and did not want you to know about it until much later.

Did you know what bipolar disorder was?

At that time, no, I didn't.

Did he tell you? How'd you find out?

I found out through his sister, who is not bipolar. I questioned him about it, and I saw some court papers that said he had his parental rights terminated. His second wife didn't want him to see his son. She said that it caused more problems in their relationship because the child was also diagnosed.

. . . He was diagnosed by a psychiatrist by court order . . . he was ADHD and bipolar and OCD [obsessive-compulsive disorder] on top of that. He and his mother both. They refused to believe that they were [bipolar].

Do you know which types of bipolar they were?

His mother was II. I can't really get the diagnosis, but they were both very bipolar.

Did he exhibit a lot of mania?

Yes. He did a lot of reckless things, and he would do things that were very dangerous. He kept an M16 gun under the bed, if that tells you anything. He also expected his mother to pay his bills because he couldn't stick to anything. He couldn't stick to a job. Then there were a lot of drama and stories and embellishments about how wonderful he was because he knew that he couldn't maintain and be like a regular person in this world.

Did you ever fear him?

Yes.

Did you think he was going to harm himself?

He told me that when his son was taken away, he tried to set his house on fire and he was going to go up with it.

Could he hold a job?

He would for a while, and then he would lose interest. Then he would screw up, and just like with me, [he thought that] the best way to get out of a relationship is to destroy it.

What advice would you give people who are in the same situation?

I think that if the person refuses to get treatment, they can be very destructive in their relationships because they don't want to admit it, especially if they lie or try to fool people. You have to get to the point where you've had enough and you know they're not going to get help. He refused to take medication, he refused to get treatment, he said therapy was a bunch of hogwash, and so I was done. I was *done*.

How long did it take you to reach that point?

After his last lie—after his last major lie—I realized that he was not going to do anything to get better and that he had the same patterns in every relationship with every woman. [My] therapist told me, "This will happen again." I found out that [after we broke up] he hurried up and got married, and she's already divorced him.

Were you able to separate the illness from the person?

In the beginning, I think he was being who he could be, but then [bipolar disorder] would take over, and he was that way long enough to get me hooked in. So that's who I fell in love with. But after I found out who he really was, I could no longer love him.

What do you know now that you wish you'd known at the start?

I think there are red flags if you've never dealt with a person with that disorder. I think I could see it coming for miles now. I think people need to really take their time getting to know anyone in a relationship, because [my ex-fiancé] could fool people for a long time. And when you're hooked in, it's too late.

Anything you wish you knew then, or now?

Well, I lived it for 3-1/2 years. I think it would be interesting to know if [medicine] can eventually do something to really, really change the trauma and the stigma of being bipolar. I think some people think it means you're so mentally ill that you're disabled.

It is *a disability.*

Well, it is, but it seems to me that the right balance of medication would help. I feel sorry for people who can't find that balance because then it's like a bad movie; you keep having reruns. I think it has to be exhausting to be that way.

Anything else you'd like to add?

It was a real nightmare at the time, but when I look back, I'm really happy I got out of it.

No-fun-for-either-of-them fact: Patty Duke, who had bipolar I, was married at one time to John Astin—Gomez on the *Addams Family* TV series (1964–66). She was diagnosed during their marriage, which was turbulent because of her extreme manic episodes. (Her book *A Brilliant Madness*; Appendix B)

S.
Past relationship

What was your relationship with the bipolar person?

We lived together for 22 years.

How long did you know her before you found out that she was bipolar?

Fifteen years.

Did you suspect it before you found out? If so, why?

I remember watching a Patty Duke bio on television and realizing that was exactly the same behavior I was seeing in my partner.

How did she find out that she's bipolar?

I think (I am not certain because I was not privy to the doctor's actual diagnosis) that [she found out] after about the second or third trip to the psych ward. She was prescribed lithium, and for a while, her moods evened out. Since she was also diagnosed with BPD [borderline personality disorder], there was a long string of drug successes and spectacular failures.

Do you know what kind of bipolar diagnosis she has?

No. I had limited interaction with her doctors. I had to go to our general physician for help. He got me to get letters from both her sister and her brother to arrange for a meeting with her psychiatrist.

Did you know anything about bipolar disorder before she was diagnosed?

Absolutely nothing.

Were you able to tell when she was in a manic/hypomanic or depressive cycle?

Wild spending on luxury items followed by depressive behavior like marathon sleeping.

Were you ever afraid of her behavior?

Yes. Most of the the abuse was mental, but some was physical.

What do you wish you'd known then about bipolar disorder? What do you wish you know now?

Mostly I wish I'd known that this was a valid illness and it wasn't my fault.

What advice would you give anyone else who's close to a bipolar person?

They are worth the trouble. Bipolars are usually very intelligent and fun and engaging when they are not in the grip of their illness.

Do you have any suggestions about what not to say to a bipolar?

"Sure, you can have my credit card." But seriously, telling them that their feelings (even if they seem wildly inappropriate) aren't valid.

Anything else you'd like to add?

[I spent] three years going every day to the hospital to visit, ignored by the doctors and the nurses. They chose not to involve me in the treatment, and I didn't even know that she was on furlough until she called for a ride. Or they'd [hospital security] call if she escaped.

[There were] countless hours waiting in the emergency waiting room due to drug overdoses, not knowing what was going on even though I was the person who brought her in.

In the '90s, there was little to no consideration given to significant others and family. I hope that has changed.

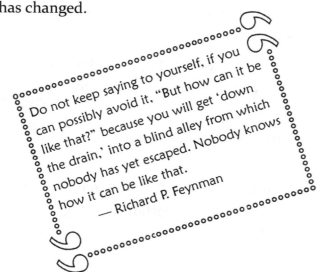

Do not keep saying to yourself, if you can possibly avoid it, "But how can it be like that?" because you will get 'down the drain,' into a blind alley from which nobody has yet escaped. Nobody knows how it can be like that.
— Richard P. Feynman

K.
Current relationship

How long have you known T.?

It's been 11 years. We started out in 2008 . . . and he was definitely in a bipolar swing at that point.

What kind of swing are you talking about: high or low?

Low. Alcohol makes him go deeply low.

How did you recognize that?

I didn't at the time. I didn't know him very well. But he was drinking, and he is totally incapacitated when he's drinking. The bipolarism, he's known about for a long time.

BP I or BP II?

I'm not sure.

If you didn't know him, would he seem different from other people, do you think?

Yeah, maybe just a little odd or eccentric, quirky. . . . There's a different resonance going on.

So he self-medicated?

[He made] an attempt at it, I think. But there were mitigating circumstances largely outside of his control. And those were the triggers. . . . As he got older, there were major life triggers that set in motion a whole other chemistry in his brain.

How high does he go? Is he out of control ever?

He has been but not anymore, because he's aware of it. . . . But back when I first knew him, it was like insanity. . . . He was just high—that kind of manic high, crazy, always laughing and hyper, and that's not his personality.

Does he experience anger?

Unexpected [fits of anger]. And then they go on a little too long. They do have a surprising, startling effect.

Do they surprise him?

I'm not sure that he's aware. I don't think he's aware of the effect. But self-awareness is a critical word.

How do you feel about all this?

For me, it's frustrating because you never know when he's really present. Sometimes it's just perfect, it's fine and normal, and we're having a conversation. But once the shift occurs, it goes on for months. I think it usually takes him time to get there mentally. . . . But he just lets himself go down that rabbit hole. I can see the arc of it. I can pretty much predict when the reset will occur. So his patterns . . . became predictable.

I would say that December through about March is the depressive part. It seems to follow that seasonal curve.

So when he's busy, he's better?

Right. That's what he realizes now: that he has to be busy, he can never drink again, because [otherwise] it's too chaotic all around.

Have you ever been afraid of him?

No. Not at all. The outbursts are loud and show frustration, but no, I've never felt afraid for my life.

Do you have any advice for people who are close to someone who has, or may have, bipolar disorder?

General advice would be that you can't take it personally, you cannot abandon the person, and you have to establish some boundaries. If I'm telling you that you seem to be bipolar or you're entering into one of your phases, accept what I'm saying, because I am actually seeing what your behavior is.

At one point, I *did* say that to him. I said, "You have to listen to what I'm saying. I see what you're doing. You're not. You're not necessarily seeing yourself." Especially if it's a long-term relationship and one you want to maintain, the person who is bipolar needs to admit it, needs to accept it, and needs to go seek medication because medication clearly has a mitigating effect.

And you need to be open to the idea that [bipolar disorder] is progressive. It keeps marching on. It's not a one-time deal.

Can you think of anything you know not to do now? Or that you'd be hesitant to do? Or anything you'd be hesitant to tell him?

I think trying to apply a rational approach in a moment when you know that this person is not necessarily rational, and then to push it, to gain your own sense of security, does not help at all.

I need to be present also. But not an enabler. And not a hostage.

In other words, the boat is rocking, and to stabilize yourself, you feel like you need to control the situation . . .

And you can't. You can't say, "Oh, by the way, you seem to be bipolar right now, and you're in your depressive mode, and can you please get a life?" It doesn't work. . . . You just kind of wait it out because you get used to that.

It resonates with you.

Oh, absolutely. You can't avoid it if you want to have a relationship with someone with this condition.

Never Ask Bipolars When They'll Get Well (and Other Big Mistakes)

When will you get well?

Are you dangerous?

Are you crazy?

Were you always crazy?

Does your brain still work?

How did you get this?

Is this why your whole family is so weird?

Do you have to get electroshock?

Aren't you glad you don't have manic depression?

(For BP IIs) Aren't you lucky you don't have the bad kind?

It's natural to want to help the bipolar to whom you're adjacent, but you won't always know what to do. Neither will the bipolar in your life always know what he or she needs. These situations have nothing to do with being bipolar-adjacent or actually bipolar; they have to do with being human.

One of the many things I loved about *Veep* was Selina's not knowing what she wanted until Gary brought it to her: a cup of tea, maybe, or the perfect shade of lipstick (Dubonnet), or a croissant with a "raspberry surprise." Selina's condition is human as it gets.

Luckily, you don't have to be a Gary. These tips (adapted from *Bipolar Disorder For Dummies*) can help you help a manic-depressive without harming either of you:

- *Set realistic expectations* for the bipolar person, the course of the illness, and the powers of medication and therapy.
- *Separate the bipolar from the disorder* by trying not to attribute all of his or her behavior to the illness.
- *Try not to take the big mood swings personally* by remembering that they're not in the bipolar's control and may not have anything to do with you.
- *Know what you can and can't do* by learning as much as possible about the disorder; being supportive instead of controlling; and accepting that you can't, and shouldn't, do everything for her or him.*
- *Prepare for crisis situations* by knowing how to recognize severe mania/hypomania or depression, having a plan of action, and storing pertinent emergency numbers on your phone.
- *Look after your own health and well-being* by taking care of yourself, having a personal support group, and letting friends or relatives help you when they offer.

* Friendly advice: Resist the temptation to be the Man/Woman of Steel, the Caped Crusader, or Captain Underpants, always swooping in to save the day. You're not the boss of us, and we might resent too many rescues. (Unless you really *are* a superhero, in which case we want to drive the Batmobile.)

More 411 Without 911

All the following organizations offer a wealth of resources online—many too many to list here. Some of these may be useful to you *and* to your bipolar friend or relative.

bpHope Magazine
- Relationships page: https://www.bphope.com and click/tap the Relationships tab
- General information: https://www.bphope.com and click/tap the About, Symptoms, and Treatment tabs

Depression and Bipolar Support Alliance (DBSA)
- Chapters and Support Groups page: https://www.dbsalliance.org and click/tap the Support tab
- For Friends and Family page: https://www.dbsalliance.org/support/for-friends-family
- Online Support Groups page: https://www.dbsalliance.org and click/tap the Support tab

International Bipolar Foundation
- Caregiver resources: http://www.ibpf.org/i-care-someone-bipolar-disorder
- General resources: http://www.ibpf.org/resources

Mental Health America (MHA)
- Find Help resources: http://www.mentalhealthamerica.net and click/tap the pertinent Find Help link
- Find Support Groups page: http://www.mentalhealthamerica.net/find-support-groups

National Alliance on Mental Illness (NAMI)
- Family Members and Caregivers page: https://www.nami.org/Find-Support/Family-Members-and-Caregivers
- NAMI Family Support Group: https://www.nami.org and search for *family support group*

National Institute of Mental Health (NIMH)
- Help for Mental Illnesses page: https://www.nimh.nih.gov/health/find-help/index.shtml
- General information about bipolar disorder: https://www.nimh.nih.gov/index.shtml and click/tap through Mental Health Information > Brochures and Fact Sheets > Bipolar Disorder

Substance Abuse and Mental Health Services Administration (SAMHSA)
- Behavioral Health Treatment Services Locator: https://findtreatment.samhsa.gov
- Understanding Bipolar Disorder Caregiver fact sheet (PDF): https://www.samsha.gov; search for *fact sheets* and scroll down
- Core Elements in Responding to Mental Health Crises fact sheet (PDF): https://www.samsha.gov; search for *fact sheets* and scroll down

Chapter 13

Bipolars: Balancing Act

Y ou've seen mostly my history in this book. I wanted to include several other bipolars' recollections, but for possibly obvious reasons, most of those I contacted didn't want to go on the record, even anonymously.

So I'm extra-grateful to T., his partner K. (who added her perspective), and C. for telling their stories.

T.
High Highs
and
Low Lows

Before diagnosis   Mine's a long story. It could have been bipolar depression [at first], or it may not have been, but when I eventually got diagnosed, I already knew.

I was diagnosed in my 20s, but that's misleading; it never really reoccurred until 2008. I might have messed around with [medication] for a year or so, and then I just didn't take any more.

I didn't really know what happened [in 2008]. I went into that super-low. Different things probably tripped it.

[Highs] make you believe you're invincible. The up, I loved, but the down put me on the couch, and I started drinking. When you're low, you want to feel different, and that's why you self-medicate.

After the second or third time of those cycles, I told people, "I've got to go to the doctor. I've got to do something, because there's something going on here."

A famous line is "I was lost in my own backyard." And I *was*.

T. was diagnosed in 2008 as bipolar after being admitted to a hospital for alcohol detox. He wasn't told, and doesn't know, whether his diagnosis was BP I or BP II.

Lithium   I've heard that this illness is ancient. The Greeks knew about it, and the Indians knew about it. They figured out that there's a naturally occurring element called lithium, and they would bathe in it or drink it. That's what I take.

Lithium is pretty basic stuff. This time, [I've taken it] six, seven, eight years. Lithium has to be managed because it's [about] balance. I don't notice or feel anything with it. The theory is if I keep my levels balanced, I won't go down very low, and I won't go up very high. It'll hold me more in the middle.

> " Bipolar disorder and alcoholism often go hand in hand. According to a couple of recent studies, 46.2 percent of BP Is and 39.2 percent of BP IIs abuse alcohol, compared with 14 percent of the general population. A separate study found that mania and alcohol abuse are 6.2 times more likely to occur together than chance would suggest. (National Institutes of Health [NIH]) "

Getting medication   *Although T. briefly took lithium in his 20s, he had trouble getting a prescription for it after his 2008 diagnosis. "When he needed it the most," K. says, "he found the right therapist" at a hospital-affiliated clinic.*

The bottom line is if you need lithium and you can't get it, and nobody's going to [write a prescription], you have to get [talk] therapy first. I had to have four classes before they'd give me the pill. I went through all the paces. It took about a month, and [because of depression] I could barely move.

Then they said, "You don't need this place. It's really not for you. What we suggest to help you is to go to your family doctor. We're gonna have *them* start issuing you lithium."

Lithium, I think you need to give about six months.

K. says, "He didn't experience any side effects, except he had to go to the doctor [for testing]. She checked him after about six months to see his blood level."

Highs and lows

I know that I have high highs. Now, we [bipolars] love the highs. Somebody told me the other day that Kanye West is bipolar, and he doesn't take his medicine when he's on a high because of the creativity.

When I'm on a high, I don't sleep that well. I wake up at 2, 3 in the morning. I've got a lot of energy. And I'm very creative. When I'm high, I touch genius. But when I go down to a low, I'm just depressed.

The last [high] was over this month; it lasted approximately 80 days. I've had [bipolar disorder] long enough that I can tell what's going on. I feel it.

But if you take care of yourself—physically, mentally, spiritually, the whole nine yards—the best you can, I think you can balance yourself to where the bipolar doesn't bounce you much. I think in the long run, you end up not swinging.

Here's the offset to that: I can be pretty good and live life pretty well, and then I won't have these swings. But life isn't as much fun. I'm having to be a middle guy, and I played higher up on the team.

Every once in a while, I still want to run off with the ball. But I'm getting to the point where I don't care anymore. Because I can't.

> In an alcohol-dependent person, either use or withdrawal may trigger bipolar symptoms because the same brain chemicals may be involved. (NIH)

Living with bipolar disorder

You can manage your own bipolar, in my opinion. You do different things, and one thing is that you don't drink. And you don't do drugs. You want to hold yourself centered and stable.

You live your life as clean as you can. You don't want stress. You want some exercise, even just walking around the block. You can't be a loner. You can't spend all your time in front of the TV. You've got to get out and see people; you can't isolate.

It's balance. You keep busy and keep healthy, and eat the right food. Exercise is a key component.

Downsides   When I'm up, and I'm rolling high, I'm running the show. Once I come down, soon I have a lot of people pushing me [because] they don't really want to accept my bipolarism.

[K. says: "Here's what you've told me. I think this is a significant thing. Let's say you've had an episode, and you feel more balanced. You're coming out of it. What you've said to me is that you wish people would not expect more of you or push you even though you seem to be normal."]

Let's say others around you realize that you're on a high. They'll back off when they see that you're in that extreme mode, maybe not asking you to do things for them. But a few months later, they should not think that you are back to normal. Because you're still not.

A lot of people have a lot of expectation. See, expectations and projections bring on resentments. [Unrealistic expectation] puts pressure on you. I recognize it.

There are [other] factors that throw you off. You could be maintaining, and then you get a week of 105 heat index. Weather can be a factor. Or you could get sick. Or you could be pushed into a trigger. Or your vehicle quits running. All kinds of factors in that low can make it worse.

For the newly diagnosed   I would say first you're gonna have to accept it and believe it, because a lot of people I know don't accept or believe it. It's just like quitting drinking or drugs: You have to hit your low first. They've got to hit their low.

Take the best care of yourself you can. You need a balance.

[K. adds: "And self-awareness. Take it seriously."]

If they take it seriously, and they take care of themselves, they won't get in the pit and can't get out. Someone has to help you out of the pit.

What you would call well periods in between [cycles] is what you seek.

Finally . . .   What else can I be [but bipolar] anyway? I am what I am. I could say that I'm blessed, because a blessed life is not an easy life.

C.
Home Safe

C.'s story begins with an almost-deadly crisis. Luckily, it doesn't end there.

Then   [One night] my youngest daughter almost got strangled by her fiancé at the time, and she called me in tears. I got into my car with a 20-gauge shotgun but no shells; I was planning on pinning him down by the throat with the shotgun.

But the police were called, and things got very real for me: I was arrested and spent the night in county jail. I saw the judge in the morning, and he ordered a doctor to get involved. That's when I was diagnosed as bipolar.

Now   I see my shrink every other month, and he keeps my bipolar II controlled with Cymbalta, Neurontin, and Abilify. I am now very even in my emotions—no more ups and downs. I don't ever want to be that woman with the shotgun again!

The hard parts   The hardest part is the shame, knowing that I hurt people before I was officially diagnosed. That is something I am going to have to live with.

Also, it really sucks relying on medication. But a friend who is also bipolar says it is no different from being diabetic and needing insulin, so I go with it. I never want to go back to the rages. The shotgun episode was by far the worst. (Who *was* that woman?) So I will take my medication faithfully for my family, my friends, and myself.

Private, not secret   Not many people know about my diagnosis, even though I was jailed and on the front page of the local newspaper. I am a very private person. But the people who matter in my life are the ones who know, and they are very supportive.

Truly blessed   Now I'm happy with my life. I live in the country; I have a great job, a wonderful family, and an awesome church and pastor. My husband and I travel as much as [our] vacation time allows. I am truly blessed!

And I hope my story can help someone else.

> The bravest are surely those who have the clearest vision of what is before them, glory and danger alike, and yet notwithstanding, go out to meet it.
> — Thucydides

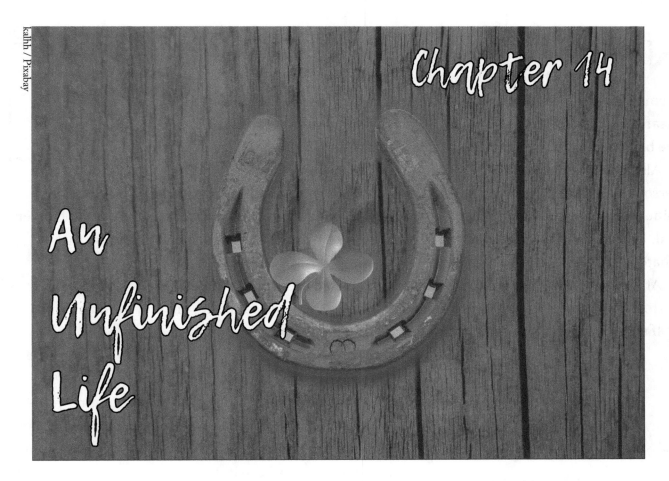

Chapter 14

An Unfinished Life

Being Irish, he had an abiding sense of tragedy, which sustained him through temporary periods of joy.
— William Butler Yeats

Being Irish (mostly), I get this on a deep level. It's perfectly Irish and perfectly bipolar wrapped into one. You could switch out *tragedy* and *joy* for mood cycles without changing a whit of Yeats's meaning. We BP IIs and/or Celtic-descended understand the *temporary* part.

Everything is temporary, of course. Only depression seems to last forever. It's been that way for me, and will be again; at least there's finally an explanation why.

Now that I know about being manic-depressive, the past makes more sense. There's been a world of damage, but much of it seems strangely beautiful now, and some of the worst mistakes (that means you, M. the First, and J., and especially H.) have made some of the best memories. I'm trying to be grateful for this.

Also, I'm learning—with the greatest reluctance—that I don't *personally* turn the crank that revolves the world, so some of what happens, good and bad, isn't mine to control. Luck matters in life. It doesn't always happen good; sometimes, it doesn't happen bad. I don't know how to be lucky. I'm only trying to nail the horseshoe open side up so that whatever luck comes in won't run out.

At the same time, I'm trying to learn to trust mixed blessings and the Mysteries. Bipolar II is both. Who knows—it may come from where all blessings and mysteries are said to come from.

If so, the gods be praised that they see me through my manic-depressive days.

> God may be subtle, but he isn't plain mean.
> — Albert Einstein

> May those who love us love us.
> And those that don't love us,
> May God turn their hearts.
> And if He doesn't turn their hearts,
> May He turn their ankles,
> So we'll know them by their limping.
> — Irish proverb

Not that there's anything *right* with that, mind you—not that anyone would take this path or thank Providence for it, given a choice. We bipolars have a mental illness. We'll always have it. It makes us very different from others. It makes the intrinsic hardness of life that much harder.

But consider the alternative.

I did—and decided that even this difficult, challenging, often-harrowing existence may still be worth seeing through.

So this bipolar life is unfinished. I have weeks, months, and years yet to be sustained by a sense of tragedy and watched over by gods who may be mad.

Nothing that follows will be perfect. What is? I'll always be manic-depressive. Can't change that. Here's one more bit of poetic Irish wisdom:

> *He, too, has resigned his part*
> *In the casual comedy;*
> *He, too, has been changed in his turn,*
> *Transformed utterly:*
> *A terrible beauty is born.*
> — Yeats (from "Easter, 1916")

You could read that this way: Even bipolar life is *meant* to change you, so you might as well let it. You might as well live.

Good luck.

Two children holding hands by some cars, photo by Irvin M. Peithmann (circa 1957) / State Library & Archives of Florida, Florida Memory, accessed August 24, 2019

Goodbipolar.

Part 6
Appendixes

Appendix A
Glossary

ADA: Americans with Disabilities Act of 1990, which (with certain restrictions) protects bipolars and other disabled people from workplace discrimination

ADHD: attention-deficit/hyperactivity disorder, encompassing the primarily inattentive type (also called *ADD*) and the primarily hyperactive-impulsive type

anticonvulsive: medication prescribed to control bipolar depression and prevent epileptic seizures

antidepressant: medication prescribed to alleviate depression

anxiety disorder: mental condition (not illness) manifesting in fear and/or anxiety

anxiolytics: antianxiety medications

ASMR: autonomous sensory meridian response; a tingling sensation in response to certain sounds

bipolar depression: an extended, severe depressive cycle in BP II

Bipolar NOS: Bipolar Not Otherwise Specified, a form of bipolar disorder with symptoms that don't fit the recognized categories; also called *Other Specified and Unspecified Bipolar and Related Disorders*

bipolar spectrum: a broad diagnostic category that includes nonbipolar disorders

black-box warning: An FDA warning about a drug's serious and/or life-threatening risks

BP I: bipolar I disorder, characterized by extreme mood swings and more mania than depression

BP II: bipolar II disorder, characterized by longer episodes of depression, milder episodes of mania, and shorter well periods than in BP I; see also *hypomania*

BPD: borderline personality disorder

CBT: cognitive-behavioral therapy; a form of psychotherapy that involves changing behaviors and thought patterns

CDC: U.S. Centers for Disease Control and Prevention

CES: cranial electrotherapy stimulation; a type of electrotherapy for mental illness

comorbid: co-occurring medical and/or psychiatric condition

CYA: a term you can look up yourself

cyclothymia: a form of bipolar disorder involving persistent symptoms too mild or short to be diagnosed as BP I or II; also called *cyclothymic disorder*

DBSA: Depression and Bipolar Support Alliance

DEA: U.S. Drug Enforcement Administration

DoL: U.S. Department of Labor

DSM-5: *The Diagnostic and Statistical Manual of Mental Disorders*, 5th Edition, published by the American Psychiatric Association

dual diagnosis: diagnosis with both a mental illness and substance abuse disorder (see also *SUD*)

ECT: electroconvulsive therapy

Ed.D.: doctor of education; an advanced degree often held by psychiatric mental-health nurses

EDMR: eye-movement desensitization and reprocessing therapy, which attempts to help patients process trauma

EEOC: U.S. Equal Employment Opportunity Commission

efficacy: a medication's ability to provide therapeutic benefits

FCC: Federal Communications Commission

FDA: U.S. Food and Drug Administration

FMLA: The Family and Medical Leave Act of 1993, which (with certain restrictions) allows up to three months' medical leave for conditions including mental illness

formulary: list of medications covered by a health insurance policy; also known as a *drug list*

genotype: a person's genetic fingerprint

HR: human resources (a terrible name, when you think about it)

hypomania: a less severe form of mania characteristic of BP II

lability: instability

LCSW: licensed clinical social worker

LGBTQ+: acronym for *lesbian, gay, bisexual, transgender, queer* (or *questioning*), and other identities

M.A. and M.S.: master of arts and master of sciences; degrees often held by nonmedical therapists

major depression: a mood disorder characterized by hopelessness and despair that persists for two weeks or more, accompanied by recognized symptoms listed in the *DSM-5* (see above); also called *clinical depression* or *major depressive disorder*

mania: a bipolar cycle during which a person is highly elated, energetic, and often reckless; characteristic of BP I

manic depression: another term for *bipolar disorder*

manic-depressive: a person who has bipolar disorder

MAOIs: monoamine oxidase inhibitors; antidepressants

MCMI: Milon Clinical Multiaxial Inventory

MHA: Mental Health America; advocacy group

mixed state: a mood episode during which a bipolar experiences both highs and lows

MMPI: Minnesota Multiphasic Personality Inventory

MSW: master of social work, a degree held by clinical social workers

Myers-Briggs Type Indicator (MBTI): a personality inventory designed to pinpoint personality type

NAMI: National Alliance on Mental Illness

NCBI: National Center for Biotechnology Information

NDMDA: National Depressive and Manic Depressive Association

NDRIs: norepinephrine and dopamine reuptake inhibitors; antidepressants

neurotransmitters: chemical agents in the brain, released by neurons, that transmit impulses throughout the brain and nervous system

NIH: National Institutes of Health

NIMH: National Institute of Mental Health

OCD: obsessive-compulsive disorder, a mental illness involving obsessive thoughts and repetitive behaviors

ODD: oppositional defiant disorder, a disorder primarily of children and teenagers characterized by anger toward and/or defiance of authority figures

OTC: over the counter

personality disorder: recurrent abnormal behavior pattern (but not a mental illness); also called *character disorder*

pharmacogenomics: study of the way that genes affect the body's ability to metabolize drugs

pharmacopoeia: an authoritative publication that describes drugs or a collection of drugs

Ph.D.: doctor of philosophy, a degree often held by psychiatrists

phototherapy: light therapy, sometimes used to treat mood cycles

prodrome: the period before a manic/hypomanic or depressive episode during which subtle symptoms occur

psychoactive: affecting the mind

psychomotor retardation: slowed movement, thought, and reactions, especially during depression

psychosis: severe detachment from reality, often with hallucinations and delusions

Psy.D.: doctor of psychology, a degree often held by psychiatrists

rapid cycling: four or more distinct manic/hypomanic and depressive episodes within a year

REM: rapid eye movement; a deep stage of sleep

R.E.M.: one of the writer's favorite bands

Riso-Hudson Enneagram Type Indicator (RHETI): a test designed to identify the taker's personality type

R.N.: registered nurse; one license held by psychiatric mental-health nurses

SAMHSA: Substance Abuse and Mental Health Services Administration

SARIs: serotonin antagonist and reuptake inhibitors; antidepressants

SCID-5: Structured Clinical Interview for DSM-5; see also *DSM-5*

scrip: short for *prescription*

serotonin syndrome: high, potentially dangerous concentration of the brain chemical serotonin in the bloodstream

serum concentration: amount of a medication in the bloodstream

SNRIs: serotonin-norepinephrine reuptake inhibitors; antidepressants

SSRIs: selective serotonin reuptake inhibitors; antidepressants

stimulant: medication that increases energy, activity, and powers of concentration

subsyndromal: symptoms not severe enough for a clinical diagnosis of a syndrome

SUD: substance abuse disorder (excessive use of alcohol, prescription and street drugs, and the like)

tetracyclic antidepressants: antidepressants that affect serotonin and noradrenaline

titration: the process of determining the optimal dose of a medication (greatest improvement in symptoms with fewest side effects)

TMS: transcranial magnetic stimulation; a type of electrotherapy for mental illness

tricyclic antidepressants: antidepressants that affect serotonin and norepinephrine

unipolar depression: major depression without the mood swings of bipolar disorder; see also *bipolar depression*

VNS: vagus nerve stimulation; a depression treatment involving electrical stimulation of that nerve

WHO: World Health Organization

Appendix B
Further

What follows is an idiosyncratic selection of resources that may be of value to you. (Books listed here are my own copies; newer editions may be available.)

Books

Bipolar Disorder

Bipolar Disorder: A Guide for Patients and Families, by Francis Mark Mondimore, M.D. (The Johns Hopkins University Press, 2006)

Bipolar Disorder For Dummies, 3rd Edition, by Candida Fink, M.D., and Joe Kraynak, M.A. (John Wiley & Sons, Inc., 2016)

A Brilliant Madness: Living with Manic-Depressive Illness, by Patty Duke and Gloria Hochman (Bantam Books, 1992)

An Unquiet Mind: A Memoir of Moods and Madness, by Kay Redfield Jamison (Vintage Books, 1996)

Archetypal Psychology and Myth

Awakening the Heroes Within, by Carol S. Pearson (HarperCollins, 1991)

The Hero with a Thousand Faces, by Joseph Campbell (Princeton University Press/Bollingen Foundation, 1972)

The Hero Within, by Carol S. Pearson (Harper & Row, 1989)

Mythology, by Edith Hamilton (Mentor, 1982)

The Portable Jung, by Carl Gustav Jung, edited by Joseph Campbell (Penguin Books, 1976)

Re-Visioning Psychology, by James Hillman (HarperPerennial, 1992)

The Soul's Code, by James Hillman (Random House, 1996)

Women Who Run with the Wolves, by Clarissa Pinkola Estés, Ph.D. (Ballantine Books, 1992)

Psychological/Personality Type Tests

Do What You Are, by Paul D. Tieger and Barbara Barron-Tieger (Little, Brown & Company, 1992)
Gifts Differing, by Isabel Briggs Myers with Peter B. Myers (Davies-Black Publishing, 1995)
Myers-Briggs Type Indicator (MBTI), https://www.themyersbriggs.com/en-US/Products-and-Services/Myers-Briggs
Riso-Hudson Enneagram Type Indicator (RHETI), https://www.enneagraminstitute.com/rheti
Strong Interest Inventory, https://www.themyersbriggs.com

There are no public-facing websites for the Milon Clinical Multiaxial Inventory (MCMI) and the Minnesota Multiphasic Personality Inventory (MMPI), both mentioned in Chapter 10.

Other Books

Anything by Carrie Fisher, but especially *The Best Awful* and *Shockaholic* (Simon & Schuster, 2004 and 2011)
A Moveable Feast: The Restored Edition, by Ernest Hemingway (Scribner/Simon & Schuster, 2009)
The Portable Dorothy Parker (Penguin Books, 1976), and not just for "Résumé"

Bipolar and ADHD Info Online

ADDitude Magazine: https://www.additudemag.com
bpHope Magazine: https://www.bphope.com
Depression and Bipolar Support Alliance: https://www.dbsalliance.org
International Bipolar Foundation: www.ibpf.org
Mayo Clinic (general health information): https://www.mayoclinic.org
NAMI: https://www.nami.org
NCBI: https://www.ncbi.nlm.nih.gov
NIMH: https://www.nimh.nih.gov/index.shtml
PsychCentral and PsychCentral Pro: https://psychcentral.com and https://pro.psychcentral.com
PubMed: https://www.ncbi.nlm.nih.gov/pubmed
WebMD: https://www.webmd.com/default.htm

Online Media

So much online programming about bipolar disorder is available nowadays that I can't listen to (or watch, or both) more than a fraction, let alone list a truly representative sample. You're on your own here. Search your favorite podcast provider, streaming service, and online video repository for more programs on this topic than *you* can listen to (or watch, or both).

As for social media, Facebook, Twitter, Instagram, Pinterest, Reddit, and Tumblr all have masses of content on bipolar disorder and other mental-health topics.

Caveat consumptor: Quality and accuracy vary.

Appendix C
Sources and Credits

Text

I drew on publicly available research from the following sources, listed here alphabetically: *ADDitude Magazine*, *American Journal of Managed Care*, American Psychiatric Association (*DSM-5*), American Psychiatric Nurses Association, CBS News, CNN.com, Depression and Bipolar Support Alliance (DBSA), Drugs.com, *Forbes*, Gallup, Gizmodo, *The Guardian*, Harvard Medical School, History Channel, Mayo Clinic, Mental Health America (MHA), National Alliance on Mental Illness (NAMI), National Center for Biotechnology Information (NCBI), National Coalition Against Domestic Violence, National Institute of Mental Health (NIHM), National Institutes of Health (NIH), NBC News, *The New York Times*, NHS England, NPR, PsychCentral and PsychCentral Pro, *Psychology Today*, U.S. Centers for Disease Control and Prevention (CDC), U.S. Drug Enforcement Administration (DEA), U.S. Equal Employment Opportunity Commission (EEOC), U.S. Food and Drug Administration (FDA), *The Washington Post*, WebMD, *The Week*, World Federation of Societies of Biological Psychiatry, and the World Health Organization (WHO).

Journals cited by some of these sources include *Acta Psychiatrica Scandinavica*, *Alcohol Research & Health*, *The BMJ*, *British Journal of Psychiatry*, *Indian Journal of Psychological Medicine*, *International Journal of Neuropsychopharmacology*, *Medical Journal of Australia*, *Psychiatry and Clinical Neurosciences*, *Psychiatry (Edgemont)*, and *Women's Health*.

Sources of small sidebar items are cited after those items.

The following material is reproduced with permission of the publishers:

- In Chapters 11 and 12, I adapted some excerpts from *Bipolar Disorder For Dummies*, 3rd Edition, with permission of John Wiley & Sons, Inc.
- The Chapter 6 quote ("Nobody understands . . .") is reprinted with permission of PsychCentral.com.

The statistics cited herein speak for themselves; the selections and interpretations are my own, as are any errors.

Art

All art used in this book except the cover photo and intro graphic is public-domain, copyright-free, and/or out of copyright. When the photographer's or artist's name is known, he or she is credited.

Some of the artwork used is licensed under the Creative Commons Attribution-Share Alike 4.0 International license (CC BY-SA 4.0; https://creativecommons.org/licenses/by-sa/4.0/deed.en), the Creative Commons Attribution-Share Alike 3.0 Unported license (CC BY-SA 3.0; https://creativecommons.org/licenses/by-sa/3.0/deed.en), or the Creative Commons Attribution-NoDerivs 2.0 Generic license (CC BY-ND 2.0; https://creativecommons.org/licenses/by-nd/2.0) and is identified as such.

All artwork is reproduced without change except for conversion of color images to black-and-white.

About the Author

K. Simpson still owns *Led Zeppelin IV* on vinyl (Chapter 7).

Printed in the USA
CPSIA information can be obtained
at www.ICGtesting.com
LVHW081103161123
763986LV00085B/2496

9 781949 290523